THE DRAGONSLAYER SERIES

DEFEATING THE DRAGONS OF THE WORLD

Resisting the Seduction of False Values

Stephen D. Eyre

With Study Questions for
Individuals or Groups

INTERVARSITY PRESS
DOWNERS GROVE, ILLINOIS 60515

InterVarsity Press is the book-publishing division of InterVarsity Christian Fellowship, a student movement active on campus at hundreds of universities, colleges and schools of nursing. For information about local and regional activities, write Public Relations Dept., InterVarsity Christian Fellowship, 6400 Schroeder Rd., P.O. Box 7895, Madison, WI 53707-7895.

Distributed in Canada through InterVarsity Press, 860 Denison St., Unit 3, Markham, Ontario L3R 4H1, Canada.

"Cat's in the Cradle" by Harry and Sandy Chapin, Copyright 1974, Story Songs, Ltd. All Rights Reserved. Issued on a most favored nation basis.

"I am . . .I said," by Neil Diamond, © 1971 Prophet Music, Inc. All Rights Reserved. Used by Permission.

Logo of dragon: Joe DeVelasco

Cover photograph: Michael Goss

ISBN 0-87784-518-2

Printed in the United States of America

Library of Congress Cataloging in Publication Data

Eyre, Stephen D., 1948-
    Defeating the dragons of the world.

    (The DragonSlayer series)
    Bibliography: p.
    1. Christianity and culture.   2. Christianity—
20th century.   3. Christian life—1960-
I. Title.   II. Series.
BR115.C8E97   1986   248.4   86-27839
ISBN 0-87784-518-2 (pbk.)

17	16	15	14	13	12	11	10	9	8	7	6	5	4	3	2	1
99	98	97	96	95	94	93	92	91	90	89	88	87				

To the people of God
who have been the channel of God's love
for me.

Lakeside Community Chapel,
Clearwater, Florida
Christ's Community Presbyterian Church,
Clinton, Mississippi

Acknowledgments

"WHAT MADE YOU THINK THAT YOU COULD WRITE A BOOK?" Nancy asked. I hadn't seen her in a couple of years. It was a good question. I had not indicated much interest in writing in previous years. Nor had I shown much aptitude. Certainly my English composition teachers in high school would be shocked to see a book with my name on it.

This book rises from a hunger to say something about God, the church and the culture in which we live. However, it would not have seen the light of day if it were not for numbers of friends who encouraged me to put my insights in writing.

I first announced the idea for the Dragons to our small group (we called ourselves The Prime Time) in the fall of 1982. I asked if I could present my ideas in a couple of weekly meetings. A couple of weeks turned into a year. Together we explored our hearts and the Scriptures and took on the Dragons. Ben Beaird, my fellow group member and prayer partner, asked me every week how my writing was coming. He was sure that the Dragons was a book when I had doubts.

I need also to thank my friends in Antiphon, our small group that succeeded Prime Time. I would bring drafts of the Dragons to our meetings and get their suggestions. Allen Cooper especially gave meticulous attention to detail that frequently made me furious and then grateful. His evaluations always forced me to put on paper what he heard me saying.

Both small groups were part of Christ's Community Presbyterian Church in Clinton, Mississippi, where our family experienced six years of spiritual growth. George Hunsburger, a church member and professor of missions at Belhaven College, was especially helpful in exploring how we transcend the values of our world. Trinity Presbyterian Church in Jackson, Mississippi, also gave their enthusiastic encouragement as well as the use of a hideaway office in which I was able to concentrate on writing.

I must also thank several friends in InterVarsity whose encouragement cost them a great deal. John Schmidt and Brad Burlingham, team members in Louisiana and Mississippi, gave up supervisory visits and the attention that staff normally expect from an Area Director. Dave Moore, my supervisor, was gracious beyond words. He too believed in me and the need to share Dragons with a broader audience. He freed me from many of my ministry obligations so that I could write. Over the past ten years he has been a soul mate as we together have sought to experience the pleasure of Immanuel, God with us.

Working with IVP has been a great experience. With only an idea I called Jim Sire, senior editor, on the phone and said, "I want to write a book." After I shared my idea there was a pause at the other end of the phone line and then the comment, "Yes, I think you have a book."

From then on I benefited from IVP's commitment to help me get my ideas on paper. Once the book was written, Denis Haack offered valuable suggestions and insights.

Last of all I must thank my family: my wife, Jackie, and our three sons, Jeremy, Chris and Justin. In many ways this book has been a family project. The boys' enthusiasm and Jackie's pointed questions forced me to sharpen my ideas. The book grows out of our experience together as we have struggled to not deny our values but to transform them and transcend them.

1
Discovering the Deforming Dragons

I was glad to receive a lengthy Christmas card from Cher. It was a newsy note, full of tidbits about what she and a few of our friends had been doing since graduation. Reading it brought back a lot of warm memories from a decade past. We all shared a sense of spiritual adventure, living with the Lord on a campus that was known for its academic excellence and its religious skepticism.

There was a strong sense that God was there with us. We felt that our lives had significance and that we were part of God's plan to make Christ known.

Reading Cher's card, I was struck by the contrast between those student years and the present. Something was missing. The sense of spiritual vitality and deeper meaning that was so tangible a few years ago was replaced by a dry, plodding faithfulness. It was as if the ghost of complacency was looming above, ready to descend.

I recognized the tone of determined obedience because I found it in myself. Even more than that, I too discovered a sense of complacency. The compelling cause of the gospel had become swallowed up in the day-to-day concerns of raising a family and coping with the never-ending details of my ministry.

Where was that sense of inner meaning? That sense of personal significance that filled my days and drove me from within? I've known it before. Yet now it was noticeably absent.

This hit me even harder because I had just completed a survey on the values and motivations of college students at campuses in the Southeastern United States. One striking discovery of the survey was that there was little internal sense of cause or duty among students. Primary motivations centered on personal enjoyment and the development of job-related skills.

Reflecting on Cher's letter, my experience and the survey, I realized that there must be subtle pressures affecting me and plenty of others as well. Almost imperceptibly I was being moved from the source of my life and ministry. Personal concerns and cultural values had pushed my sense of call and cause into the back seat.

A Hunger for Meaning

I was converted to Christ during the midsixties when the Beatles were singing, "All you need is love," Bob Dylan was telling the world that the times were "achangin'," and we were promised that when you go ". . . to San Francisco, you're going to meet a whole generation, with a new explanation. . . ."

I was in college during the protest years of the Vietnam War. I had long hair, played guitar in a music group, and was excited and enticed by the sense of electricity that filled the air. There seemed to be the promise of a new way of life full of justice, love and freedom. I wanted so much to be a part of all that was happening around me.

But something was wrong. With all the singing and talk about hope and freedom, I felt like an outsider. I was too short and too heavy, too, too, well, . . . I lacked something. Maybe my hair wasn't quite long enough. I could never quite get up the nerve to plunge into drugs. Or maybe I didn't own the right guitar. While everyone else seemed to be in, I always felt out. And out was the worst thing I could possibly be.

So when I was confronted with the call of Jesus Christ, I was a prime candidate. I resisted for a year, but he was persistent. And when I was converted, there it was—meaning, significance, cause—all that I was looking for in a relationship with my Creator. What they were singing about on the radio, what everyone was talking about, I found through spiritual rebirth. Knowing Christ, being taken into a vital church, I knew that I was really in. My life was transformed.

Those early years following my conversion were active ones that marked me for life. I shared my faith with my friends. I couldn't wait to tell them that the sense of anticipation in the air was an illusion. The substance was in Christ and in the Scriptures. I had a cause that filled my life and welled up from within. Several of us started a prayer meeting that grew from a student's apartment to a "happening" or a "rap session" of a couple of hundred on the beach.

Following graduation from college I went on to seminary. During those years I sang in Christian coffee houses and started a high-school youth group. Upon graduation from seminary it was natural for me to continue working in the ways that God had been using me, so I joined Inter-Varsity Christian Fellow-

ship staff. I was anxious to share with students the good news
of meaning and significance that I found since I assumed they
were looking for meaning and significance too.

That's how I got to know Cher. She was a student leader in
one of the IVCF chapters I worked with. Even in the mid-sev-
enties, that sense of cause and duty among students was waning
but was not yet dead. Together the students and I lived and
ministered in the name of Christ.

But now the culture has shifted. Students no longer have that
internal drive for some bigger cause. The issues on campus today
revolve around good times, good grades and hopes for finding
a good job. It can be discouraging when you try to bring the
power of the gospel into such a climate. But more than that, I
find it dangerous. I have discovered that I am not immune. Even
while believing that I am being true to my calling, I find that
personal concerns and job advancement are at the center of my
life.

But such an approach to life is not limited to the campus. The
campus is just a reflection of our society as a whole. The craving
for personal peace and affluence afflict us all. Even while the
starving millions in Africa, the oppression of apartheid and other disasters all tug at our consciences, the message of the media,
the pressures of the job and the battle of the budget (personal
and national)—in short, the institutions of our world and our
own perceived needs sing a siren's song of superficiality. The
message of God's offer of life to a fallen world loses its impelling
force and the church, like the rest of the culture, is pulled into
a treadmill life going nowhere.

Fighting on the Wrong Front
After my conversion, I transferred from a state school to a Christian college. I was anxious to understand the Scriptures and

apply them. What better place to do that than a Christian college? One of the first things I learned when I went there was that I must not be worldly. Being worldly was the ultimate sin. I had to cut off my long hair, had to agree not to go to movies, had to wear socks with my shoes and had to make sure my sideburns did not grow below my ears. It was important to do this for my "witness." I had to show that as a Christian, I was different from the world. All this seemed a little strange to me, but if that was what Christians were supposed to do, then I was willing to go along.

In a couple of years, as I began a beach ministry, I started hanging around with those who appeared worldly and allowed my hair to inch over my collar. I soon ran into trouble with the college administration. I was looking too much like the world and spending too much time with worldly people. Never mind that I was sharing the gospel with some of those worldly folks in significant ways. I was no longer looking like a Christian nor acting as they felt a Christian should act.

In my spiritual journey since those days at the Christian college I have come to understand worldliness in very different ways. I still agree with my friends at the college that worldliness is bad, very bad. But I'm convinced that their definition of worldliness misses the point. It is preoccupied with microethics, focusing on limited areas of personal behavior and dress.

While we fight the battle on the wrong front, the real forces of worldliness occupy the church. Spiritual concerns give way to cultural ones. Prayer gives way to busyness. Ministry gives way to organization and administration. Earning a living displaces a sense of a vocation from God. In short, cultural values that are contrary to everything the church stands for casually invade our lives. There is a quiet capitulation. We become worldly by default.

Observers of American life have noted the religious, even Christian beliefs of the American people. In contrast to England or Europe, America is very religious. One study discovered that there were 25 million people involved in home Bible studies each week. Another discovered that 80% of Americans believe that Jesus Christ is God or the Son of God, while 53% say that religion is a very important part of their lives.[1] How then do we account for the rise in drug abuse, in teen-age suicides, in poverty, in abortions and in sexual promiscuity? If the church were acting as the salt and light that Jesus expected it to be, wouldn't we notice the effect?

The Dragons
The cause of this problem is an unperceived but fatal case of worldliness. While being preoccupied with our microethics, we have not faced the invasion the world has thrown against us on another front. Certain cultural values are particularly strong and absolutely deadly for the church. On the surface they don't appear to be ungodly. In fact, we may adopt them as a way of expressing our faith. But they are transforming and deforming our faith and practice. I have a name for these values. I call them the Dragons of the World.

I have identified six Dragons:

Materialism: Matter is all that matters.

Activism: Life is to be filled with action.

Individualism: We can depend on no one but ourselves.

Conformism: Recognition by others is a necessity.

Relativism: It doesn't matter what you believe, as long as you believe something.

Secularism: Religion is all right in its place.

These six values are as American as apple pie. We drink them with our mother's milk, we learn them along with our ABCs, and they fill our minds as we hum the tunes of our favorite songs. They form the elements of the cultural atmosphere in which we live and breathe.

The Dragons have power over us because we believe that by embracing them we can achieve personal value. They are the internal guides we follow believing that if we live by them our lives will be satisfying and fulfilling.

Materialism prompts us to think, "I am what I own."

Activism encourages us to believe that, "I am what I do," or "I am what I produce."

Individualism leads us to believe that, "I am self-sufficient."

Conformism makes us think that, "I am who others recognize me to be."

Relativism suggests that, "I am whatever I choose to believe."

Secularism declares that, "I am sufficient without God."

These worldly values offer us the way to achieve and measure our worth. The Dragons make us insatiable pursuers of an illusion of personal worth. We can never achieve such value by conforming to their demands. A genuine sense of worth comes from a spiritual knowledge. It's something we know only because God puts it inside us.

These values bring desolation to the church in a quiet transformation. Cloaking themselves in Christian terminology the Dragons conform us to the world. We may believe that we are doing our best to live the Christian life when in fact we are only being good citizens.

The Dragons are screens through which biblical truth must pass and in the process is changed. Jesus' promise of an abundant life becomes the gospel of material prosperity. A consuming career driven by activism outside the church becomes a consuming ministry inside the church. And Sunday, a day set aside to strengthen us to live with God throughout the week, becomes the religious island in our lives from which we shove off to live six days in which he is only a distant memory.

The Dragons are attractive, if we are honest about it. They offer the illusion of being culturally successful while being religiously respectable. Personally, it's hard to resist the promise that God has a wonderful plan for my life which includes a large house, a beautiful family and a large regular income. Who wants to believe anything else? It's what we want to hear and we will gladly follow anyone who offers it to us in the name of God. Any church who proclaims the Dragons can expect to grow. It's the American way.

God's people in every age are likely to succumb to their own set of Dragons. Whether it is Israel facing surrounding idolatry or the Medieval church facing the god of reason, there has always been a pressure to accept surrounding cultural values. The result is deformed religion. Israel became idolatrous and the Medieval church became rationalistic. In our own time the Dragons offer a deformed value system:

Materialism: a deformed view of the world.

Activism: a deformed view of work.

Individualism: a deformed view of self.

Conformism: a deformed view of others.

Relativism: a deformed view of truth.

Secularism: a deformed view of God.

These values comprise the fabric of the world we live in. While the Dragons devastate us, they are not totally evil. They are fallen and must be redeemed. They are deformed God-given values. They are biblical values which have become ungodly.

Without biblical values the people of God have no banks to define the channel through which the Spirit of God can flow fresh, clean and deep. The church that is invaded by the Dragons loses its ability to call a bent world to repentance. There is no witness to God's redemptive kingdom. The Christian who lives by the Dragons will experience an inner hollowness and know little of true spiritual reality.

How can we be in the world and not of it? How can we not be conformed to the world but instead be transformed? The apostle Paul gives us the answer in Romans 12:2—we are to be renewing our minds. The values that come from God must transform the cultural values that I have so deeply embraced.

Touching the Beasts

Before we can become what we should be, we must take a hard look at who we really are. We have to start, therefore, by facing the presence of the Dragons in our lives. My six-year-old son has a book entitled, *There Are No Such Things as Dragons*. The story is worth repeating.[2]

One morning, a magic dragon appears in Billy's room. He is a cute little fellow, eager and frisky. As Billy gets out of bed the dragon hops on a chair and wags its tail. Curious and startled, Billy runs downstairs to ask his mother about this strange dragon.

His mother scoffs, "There are no such things as dragons." This puts Billy in a tight spot. Here is this dragon that has followed him downstairs and is now sitting on the kitchen table. What can he say?

The startled mother, who now also sees the dragon, has put herself in a tight spot as well. What should she say now that she has declared that dragons don't exist? She decides to stick with her denial. After all, everyone knows that dragons are not real.

The policy of denial doesn't work too well for Billy and his mom. As she puts pancakes on the breakfast table for Billy, the dragon eats them. The dragon is a rude little fellow and Billy and his mom both watch as it enjoys Billy's breakfast. Billy only got one of the pancakes.

Things go from bad to worse. Little by little the dragon grows throughout the day. Both Billy and his mom ignore the dragon as best they can, walking around it as they move from room to room. However, it seems that the more they ignore it, the bigger it grows. Toward the end of the afternoon the dragon has grown so large that it fills the whole house and begins to lift it off the foundation. By now even the neighbors can see the dragon and a crowd gathers to see Billy's house full of a dragon.

Something must be done. Even though his mom is still denying that dragons exist, Billy makes a decision. Although he knows that there is no such thing as a dragon, he tentatively reaches out his hand to touch and stroke the dragon's side. Suddenly a strange thing happens. The dragon starts to shrink. In a brief time the gigantic dragon has shrunk back to the cute little creature Billy first saw in his room that morning.

After everything is back under control and all the neighbors have gone, Billy's mother makes a reluctant admission. "Perhaps there really are such things as dragons."

The story's point? Denial is the wrong policy. Let's not pretend that there are no such things as dragons. If we are going to escape the world's values that dominate our lives, we must face them. By looking at them, by reaching out and touching them, we can begin the battle to defeat them. By examining them in the light of God's Word, the history of the church and by purposely submitting them to God, they can be transformed into godly values.

Discernment and Detachment

One of the spiritual disciplines of the early church was discernment. It was a gift and skill by which one could perceive the subtle shades that separated truth from error. More than ever, we need this gift today. Just recognizing the Dragons is a difficult task. I like the way Eugene Peterson puts it, "World is an atmosphere, a mood. It is nearly as hard for a sinner to recognize the world's temptations as it is for a fish to discover the impurities in the water. There is a sense, a feeling that things aren't right . . . but just what it is eludes analysis."[3] Since we are immersed in the values of our world it is hard to see the degree to which they possess us.

Throughout this book you will see an approach to truth that calls for looking at two sides of a truth, sides which are often viewed as contradictory. I am convinced that we must learn to think differently if we are to face effectively the values of the world in which we live. We can't eradicate these false values, but we can learn to transform them.

Another discipline of the early church that we need is detachment. We learn to let go of the world so that we may draw closer to God. Detachment is a task I have been struggling with for several years now. I have found it difficult beyond words. As I have discovered the depth of the Dragons in my own life, I have gone through dark days and periods of deep depression.

During one of my daily quiet times of prayer and study, I was reflecting on the degree to which I was driven to be successful in ministry. In my discussion with God over what I should do to let go, I had a sense of being called to die. It seemed so real, this call to die, that I was shaken to the very core. In the weeks that followed, every weakness and fissure in my personality seemed to break loose. My whole identity was tied up in being successful, and death was the only way out.

Over a period of time God has brought a healing, and I do seem to be less driven. But I found myself afraid of God. I'm not sure that I want to die in order to be free. Yet I am not willing to settle for a shallow superficial faith. I want a sense of inner meaning, an inner drive that gives me a focus for living.

A Quest

If you too find a desire to tame the Dragons, to find values beyond the values of our world, then I invite you to come on a quest. Put on the spiritual armor and venture forth as the knights of old. I don't offer immediate success. Instead I want to provide an approach, a few tools, a way to begin. How the battle actually goes is between you and God.

In each of the next six chapters we will look at one Dragon and some of its manifestations both in the world and in the church. Then I will suggest a biblical value that should replace it, a spiritual discipline that will help us grow and finally what results we should expect to see in our lives when we are experiencing renewal in a certain value.

Our task, as God's people in the world, is not to deny or suppress the culture in which we live, but to transform it. I am convinced that the world is not inherently bad. It's just fallen like everything else. If we look to the quality of our own lives and the quality of the church, we will have an eternal impact. We can transcend the culture and be a transforming agent in our world.

For Individuals or Groups

1. The Dragons are a primary cause of worldliness in the church. How many of the Dragons mentioned in the chapter do you recall without paging back to look?

2. Worldliness, according to my college friends, focused on dress codes. Prior to reading this chapter, how would you have described worldliness?

3. Having read this chapter, how would you describe worldliness?

4. The struggle for identity resulted in my need for the gospel. What needs and desires prepared you to respond to Jesus?

5. I lost a healthy focus on Jesus Christ when I became overly concerned with my family and ministry. What sort of pressures compete with Jesus Christ for your allegiance?

6. A primary reason the Dragons have power over us is that they offer themselves as a way to achieve personal value. How do you think each of the Dragons offer us personal worth?

7. Which of the Dragons do you think is most active in your life? Explain.

8. Discernment and Detachment, two spiritual disciplines of the early church, are suggested as ways to begin to cope with the Dragons. Mention ways in which you think they might be helpful in your life.

9. As you prepare to read the rest of the book, in what sort of ways would you like it to be helpful to you?

2
The Dragon of Materialism
Spiritual Faith in a Physical World

I confess. I like to listen to rock and roll music. Maybe it's because of my background—having played in a band. But I believe that there is more to it than that. By listening to it I learn something about where the culture is and where it is moving. One song gives an excellent summary of one of the Dragons and its effects. The refrain declares that we are living in a material world and boldly declares a materialistic approach to life. The backup singers echo the refrain about this materialistic world in the background with a machinelike metallic chant.

The thought expressed by a pop idol like Madonna in the song "Material World" may seem trite and satirical, but it is the same one Carl Sagan expressed in the book, *Cosmos*, "The Cosmos is all there is or was or will be."[1]

Materialism is a dominant cultural value, and everyone is willing to admit it. It is also hard to resist. The Dragon is everywhere. His message is transmitted by our institutions. The government is preoccupied with economics, our media encourages consumption and our universities equip us not just to learn but to earn.

The message of the Dragon of Materialism is repeated daily in a thousand different ways: "Buy, purchase, own." One study estimated that by the time the average teen-ager graduates from high school he or she will have seen 350,000 commercials.[2]

We will feel better about ourselves, we are told, if we own more. If we buy the right car, own a home in the right neighborhood, buy designer clothes, use the right toothpaste or whatever, then our problems will be over. Success, peace of mind and happiness will come to us—if only we will own. Under the blitz of the Dragon, we come to believe that our identity is tied up in what we possess. We come to think, "I am what I own." We become what we have been labeled, "Consumers."

Matter Is All That Matters

How do we live with the abundance of material goods that surround us? I struggle with this. I like what I have, and even feel like a little more wouldn't hurt. My house could be larger since we really do need more space for three growing boys. We are under a lot of pressure right now and some extra money for a little vacation would help.

As I write this chapter I am in the process of buying a new family car. How ironic! We do need a new car. Our third child has just been born and our old Chevette has 125,000 miles on it. Yet as I write about the dangers of preoccupation with the abundance of possessions, I am preoccupied. I am making a purchase for which I will be paying for the next four years. It will stretch our budget to the limit.

As I struggle with this I remind myself that possessions are not wrong or evil in themselves. After all, God made the world for us to live in and enjoy. Nor can I ever draw a line and say, this much is all right and anything more is ungodly. That approach leads to a dangerous legalism. We must find an inner compass that can guide us through the numbing smog in which we are all engulfed. We must find a harness that can tame this Dragon who enchants us.

The way materialism comes to occupy our hearts can be subtle. Initially we want to provide for ourselves and our family. The "standard package" is a three-bedroom house with central heating/air conditioning, two bathrooms, a dishwasher and garbage disposal. One car is a necessity, perhaps two. Yet to sustain such a standard lifestyle requires a great deal of energy from most of us. Usually the husband and wife both have to work. Living to work in order to buy becomes the family preoccupation.

After all, what is wrong with seeking to realize the American dream? Isn't it our right? But after all our effort, we have little time or energy left to consider the spiritual aspects of life. While believing there is more to life than owning and possessing, buying and possessing becomes the hub of our lives. The Dragon of Materialism moves into our hearts and unpacks his bags.

There is a fascinating tension created by materialism. Those characterized as Yuppies in the middle eighties were not flattered by their media image—a devotion to comfort, owning all the best things. But once the creed of the Dragon becomes the creed of our hearts, living to buy becomes a dominant part of life. The extent of the tension of materialism was illustrated from me in this amazing sentence in *Pathfinders* by Gail Sheehy. "When two thousand young men were asked to spell out their greatest concerns for the future, they expressed two major fears in equal weight—and absolute contradiction; fear of not having enough money, and fear of being locked in by the constant pursuit of money."[3]

The Gospel of Prosperity

The Dragon of Materialism has moved into the church in blatant ways. A large segment of Christians believe that God's blessings mean material prosperity for all who ask for them. The gospel, beneath the flame of this Dragon, becomes the gospel of Prosperity.

Appealing to the materialistic infection of our hearts one author writes, "Prosperity is yours! It is not something you have to strive to work toward. *You Have A Title Deed to Prosperity.* Jesus bought and paid for your prosperity just like He bought and paid for your healing and your salvation."[4] Or as another characterized it, "God's got it, I can have it, and by faith I'm going to get it."[5]

"How can these people honestly believe this?" I think to myself when I read about or hear a preacher of material prosperity. "Don't they see what the Scriptures say about the choice between serving God or Money?" However, I must confess that they are only saying explicitly what I want to believe. I just don't have the nerve to admit it. Deep down inside I just know that if I believe the right way and do the right things God is going to give me every physical thing I desire.

The church for most of its two thousand years has warned against the dangers of materialism. Bernard of Clairvaux wrote in the thirteenth century, "Money no more satisfies the hunger of the mind than air supplies the body's need for bread."[6] The Puritan William Perkins wrote that if "we intend only to get wealth, we . . . set bars on heaven's gate and load ourselves with burdens that make us unable to pass."[7]

Stacey Woods, the founder of Inter-Varsity Christian Fellowship, wrote, "A Christian must realize that material possessions have no permanent value. Supply and demand, the rise and fall of the stock market, changes in taste and fashion, the movement of society and the inevitable process of decay and obsolescence make much of what we have of temporary value. . . . How easily we citizens of heaven, secure in Christ Jesus find our imagined security in earthly things!"[8]

The Dangers

Most discussions about materialism center on developing a simple lifestyle. Should I buy a new record or tape when I already have a shelf full? Should I trade in my car on a new one or wait until it is completely falling to pieces? These are variations of, "How much is too much?" And they are important to ask. But they miss the point when it comes to dealing with materialism and its effects. Whether we are talking about having a little or a lot, we are still talking about physical things.

The flip side of the Gospel of Prosperity is the Gospel of Simple Living. For a period in my life I reacted to the materialism of the world and the church by refusing to buy much of anything. Authentic Christians, I thought, should be committed to owning as little as possible. Living in the most inexpensive housing available, owning a limited wardrobe and an old car were what I considered Christian essentials. At one time I even refused to buy a washing machine and dryer even when we had two children in diapers. While my wife, Jackie, was spending every other day at the laundromat, a couple of family friends took me aside for a frank talk on caring for my family. As I struggled with the issue of materialism, I discovered that I was still being materialistic. I was measuring my spirituality and the spirituality of others by how much or how little they owned.

The real problem of materialism is that it blinds us to the

spiritual aspects of reality. It has been said that Malcolm Muggeridge observed, "Once Christians let go the spiritual, the game is up."

Materialism is dangerous because it destroys the spiritual roots of our lives. One of the things I like about the song "Material World" is the way it illustrates the impact of materialism. The people singing the refrain in the background sound like monotonous robots—machines with no soul. When a scientist like Carl Sagan writes from a materialistic perspective, making pronouncements about the universe, it can seem profound. But something intangible, but absolutely necessary for life, is lost.

While we struggle with the slippery question of "How much is too much?" we overlook what affluence does to us. The Dragon of Materialism leads us to become preoccupied with the material side of life. All our time, energy and thought are focused on the physical aspects of life. We become practical materialists. We know that there is more to life, but the way we live shows that we have adopted the creed of the Dragon of Materialism, "Matter is all that matters."

But let's face the issue correctly. Materialism obscures our grasp of reality. It destroys the capacity for spiritual faith and perverts the way we are supposed to live before God in his world.

Materialism blunts a living faith. A vibrant sense of the presence of God becomes dead orthodoxy. The reality of the Christian life becomes a shadow. Our experience of life in Christ becomes hollow. Our knowledge of God becomes empty. If we can't see it, taste it, touch it, smell it or measure it, then we doubt that it's real; therefore, we come to doubt that God is real.

The filters of materialism place God at a distance. Without spiritual substance to our faith, learning about God substitutes for knowing God. Spiritual nourishment from the Scriptures becomes confused with the accumulation of Bible knowledge.

We may attend Bible conferences, listen to great preachers, read Christian books, learn a system of doctrine and accumulate commentaries. Yet with all our study, there is no illuminating combination of the Word and Spirit. While we gain more knowledge of Scripture, infected by materialism, we come out losers.

As we become aware of a dryness in our souls, we may conclude that what we need is more emotion mixed into our faith. But emotional reality is not the same as spiritual reality, and we are still left with a strained and futile effort to know God and live an authentic Christian life.

Worldly Salvation

Jesus, knowing what materialism does to us, warned against believing that our lives consist of an abundance of possessions. He told a rich young ruler that eternal life was only available to him if he sold all he had and then followed (Mk 10:17-22). He warned the disciples that it was easier for a rich man to enter the kingdom of heaven than it was for a camel to enter through the eye of a needle (Mk 10:23-25). He warned against storing up treasures on earth (Mt 6:19). He warned that one could gain the whole world and in the process lose his own soul (Mt 16:26).

Despite the warnings, the infection of materialism is so pervasive that even those of us who don't consciously believe in a gospel of material prosperity live it in a subtle way. Don't we measure the blessing of God by the balance in our checkbook? Don't we evaluate the success of a ministry by the size of its building? Don't we judge the power of a church by the size of its budget? (If we are really spiritual, we look at the size of the missions budget.)

It is hard for spiritual riches to compete with material ones. On a daily basis, I must admit, I am more preoccupied with working to put money in the bank than I am with following

Jesus' admonition to store up treasure in heaven.

Remember the game of Monopoly? The object is to go around the board in order to buy property and earn money. As the game progresses, money and deeds begin to be monopolized by one or two players. Those who are getting monopolies are having a great time and in no hurry for the game to end. However, if you happen to have only a few deeds and little money, the game begins to drag on and on. You begin to look forward to the end so you can get on with something else. Likewise, as long as we have hope that we can win in this life, the promise that we will have blessings in the heavenlies, seems to lack something (Eph 1:3).

Jesus rebuked the church at Laodicea for its material affluence and its spiritual ignorance. Surely he rebukes us. "You say, 'I am rich; I have acquired wealth and do not need a thing.' But you do not realize that you are wretched, pitiful, poor, blind and naked" (Rev 3:17).

Recovering the Spiritual

What about the spiritual? How is this unseen reality a part of life?

There is much about the spiritual that is unknown. Nowhere in Scripture is it described. The focus is first on *who* and only afterward on *what* the spiritual is. We don't know what spirit is, nor do we know the exact way that the spiritual is involved in our physical world. These questions, while interesting, are not important from a biblical perspective. The important thing to know about the spiritual is that God is Spirit, and that he has made a world that involves a dynamic interaction between both the spiritual and material.

The spiritual is where we meet God is his world. Communion with him is spiritual communion. God draws us to himself by the Spirit, and by his Spirit opens our minds so we can under-stand his Word. We are to pray "in the Spirit" and give praise to God with spiritual hymns and songs (Eph 4:18-19).

Essential benefits that God has provided for us in Christ are spiritual. God "has given us new birth into . . . an inheritance that can never perish, spoil or fade—kept in heaven for you" (1 Pet 1:4). He has redeemed us from sin and cleansed us by the blood of Christ—both spiritual blessings.

The life of the church is a spiritual life. Growth comes from the Spirit. Ministry within the church requires spiritual gifts. Likewise personal growth in holiness comes from the Spirit and the mature Christian is characterized as being spiritual (Gal 5:16-18, 22-25).

There is much more that could be written about the spiritual from Scripture. Morton Kelsey writes that out of 7,957 verses in the New Testament, 3,874 of them have something to say about one or more various experiences of the Spirit.[9] But my purpose is not to do an exhaustive study. Rather it is to encour-age us to cultivate a new awareness. We must learn to think in terms of the spiritual.

On New Year's Day last year I was sitting in a pizza parlor with a large-screen TV and was rooting for my team during one of the bowl games. When there was a break in the action I looked around the room wondering how many people had a relation-ship with God. I began to prayerfully reflect on ways I could share with someone next to me. As I prayed, I began to wonder how many people in the room knew they had souls. This may seem strange, but think about it. Don't we think of our inner life as essentially psychological and emotional? The soul seems like an antiquated concept belonging to previous centuries. And then I began to reflect on my awareness of my own soul. How much of the spiritual movements inside me have I attributed to emotional turmoil or heartburn?

This led me to see how materialistic my approach to evangelism had become. I frequently present the gospel as a means of emotional healing and or help for troubles, which it is . . . to a point. But I am embarrassed to admit that I have not been comfortable offering Jesus as the One who saves souls and opens the way to heaven. Nor do I think that those with whom I share would be attracted by such an offer. The screen that this Dragon has placed over our minds leads us to dismiss such an approach as only "otherworldly" or "pie in the sky bye and bye."

Material and Spiritual

As we sense the dryness of our souls, there is a new hunger for Christian spirituality surfacing in the church. At a recent conference of Presbyterians in Mississippi, several of the speakers referred to the practice of meditation and to how they were recovering the spiritual in their lives. Between sessions, as hungry enthusiasts, we traded names of authors whose writings were opening fresh springs of spiritual life for us.

In this renewed look at the spiritual, if we are to find the spiritual nourishment that we long for, we must exercise discernment. The experience and knowledge of spiritual reality creates a dynamic tension in our lives. We must learn to live in the visible and the invisible, in the spiritual and the physical.

This is not an easy task. Just as we are tempted to become preoccupied with the material in our own world, there are those in the past that have become preoccupied with the spiritual at the expense of the physical. Christians in other ages have been characterized as people whose sole concern was escaping the material world and arriving safely in heaven.

That is not Christian spirituality. That is a false spirituality which does not come from the Scriptures. God is the Creator of heaven AND earth. Jesus is Lord of heaven AND earth, of the visible AND the invisible. In the lordship of Jesus Christ, both aspects of God's creation find their unity. The very mystery of God's will is "to bring all things in heaven and on earth together under one head, even Christ" (Eph 1:10).

I have learned to think of the interaction of the spiritual and the physical as a dynamic tension. This is a difficult thing to do. None of us like to live in tension. But it is better than living in error. The following diagram is a help to me in keeping the tension in balance.

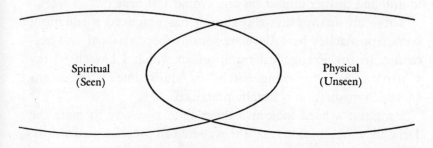

Figure 1. The Spiritual and the Physical

The challenge is to live in the intersection of the two ellipses. As long as we live in the middle we are living and thinking as we should. However, when we are pulled to either side in the extreme, then we depart from biblical truth.

Over the centuries Christians have developed and practiced spiritual disciplines as a means of seeking the balance. It is not enough to know that we are spiritually dull and need to grow. Nor will going to church once or even three times a week be sufficient. We must do something that will regularly refocus our energy and thought. We need to learn spiritual disciplines that cultivate our souls and open our spiritual eyes and ears.

Meditation

Meditation has been a foundational spiritual discipline throughout the history of the church. It is a way of looking past the
material, or perhaps through material, to see God as spiritually
present in his world.

In meditation we focus our minds. Jim Packer describes meditation as "an activity of holy thought, consciously performed in
the presence of God, under the eye of God, by the help of God,
as a means of communication with God. Its purpose is to clear
one's mental and spiritual vision of God and let his truth make
its full and proper impact on one's mind and heart."[10]

There are many ways the church has practiced meditation;
some approaches have been mystical, others rational and academic. In the Evangelical tradition, in which I have lived my
Christian life, a "morning watch," or "quiet time" is the means
by which meditation is usually practiced.

I suggest a hard look at a quiet time as a way to tame the
Dragon of Materialism and the way we can practice meditation.

But wait!

As soon as I say quiet time, some are going to miss the point.
"I know what that is," some will say, "I have them all the time.
How is that going to help me face materialism when I have been
having them most of my Christian life and it doesn't seem to
have made much difference?"

What I have discovered is that even our quiet times have been
affected by the Dragon of Materialism. We have lost the spiritual
experience of time with God and have turned it into a time full
of routines—15 minutes of Bible study, 10 minutes of reciting
our shopping list of prayer requests and then 5 minutes of Scripture memorization. And then we wonder why our quiet times are
so dry! We are not having a quiet time as a spiritual discipline,
we are having a quiet time full of techniques. We have developed

a relationship with routines not a relationship with God. How mechanical!

Many of us have also been warned to avoid looking for any feelings when we have a quiet time. "Don't look for experience," we are told. "Watch out that you don't focus on feelings." Certainly there is wisdom in this caution. But I believe that in our day and time we miss something. Spiritual interaction with God is an experience. It involves our minds, our emotions and our spirits. When we are told to watch out for feelings, in our materialized world that translates into, "It should be only an intellectual experience." On the contrary, we should not be afraid to let our quiet time be a subjective experience. When we meet God, what other kind of experience could we possibly have?

We should be cautious, however. We don't want a subjective experience only. Our personal experience with God must be rooted in the Scriptures and shared with God's people. Again we must balance a dynamic tension.

Now down to specifics. In a quiet time we set aside time every day where we can say, "Stop!" to the demands that are part of our daily routine and focus on the Lord who is with us. We develop a practice of being with our Lord in a quiet, intimate way. Quiet time is more than Bible study and more than prayer and more than reading a devotional guide. It is a place and a space in our lives where we can be with God. In a quiet time the focus is not first of all on what we do, but on Who is with us. Once we have created a space in our lives to listen to the Spirit and nourish our souls, then we can learn to grow in Bible study, prayer and other spiritual disciplines that we might find helpful.

While a quiet time is a basic spiritual discipline, it is not easy. Almost everyone I know who has a regular quiet time struggles with it, including myself. It is so difficult to be quiet. From the time we get up until we go to bed we are surrounded by unceasing activity and are immersed in the noise of people, radios or television. Getting up early in the morning we feel the pressure of our schedule and impending commitments. Our days are filled with responsibilities. By evening, we are usually too tired for a quiet time and fall asleep if we sit still for long.

But no matter what obstacles we may face, we need to find some place where we can be quiet and alone with our Lord. Spiritual sensitivity cannot be developed in any other way. My father-in-law uses his lunch time, staying in the office when everyone has gone out to eat. Perhaps a mother with young children can find time after the kids have been sent off to school. As a student, I found a slot in the morning between classes to be a great time. My favorite way to have a quiet time now is to stop at a McDonald's on the way to my office. I sit in a back booth with a cup of coffee and my Bible and a pad to write on. Whatever your situation, with determination and creativity, you can find some place to be quiet with God.

Finding a quiet place to be with the Lord is not only a problem of schedule. Becoming quiet inside ourselves is even more of a problem. As soon as I stop being busy outwardly, I find that I am busy inwardly. My mind is full of the things I need to do and should have done but didn't—people to call, groceries to pick up, errands to run, letters to write. The list is endless.

When I am quiet enough to hear, someone inside of me wants to know, "Why didn't I say what I felt when I was given that assignment that I didn't have time for?" Or I'm asked, "How am I going to deal with resentment because family demands precluded the weekend football game?" Sitting quietly I begin to wonder, "How do I really feel about being passed up to lead that important committee at church?"

Whatever your questions, don't stuff them back in the box and put them on the shelf. The secret to becoming quiet is to pay attention to these little voices. Pay attention to them. Even focus on them. Write them down. Pray about them. Wait and listen for what God might be saying about each one. It is in the midst of these frustrations and suppressed feelings the Lord meets us. The quiet time is the time and place to put these things before the Spirit and to deal with them in prayerful reflection.

When practiced in this way a quiet time becomes a place of spiritual communion with God. No longer is it only a time filled with techniques and routines. As we lift up our daily struggles and concerns to the Lord, we enter into a spiritual dialog with God that allows him to confront us, guide us and comfort us. We find quiet and nourishing rest in God's presence as we give these innermost concerns to him.

Seeing the Banquet

The essence of Christian spirituality is faith. Faith is "the assurance of things hoped for, the conviction of things not seen" (Heb 11:1 RSV). The heroes of the faith listed in Hebrews 11 were people with a spiritual vision who knew "that they were aliens and strangers on the earth . . . they were longing for a better country—a heavenly one" (Heb 11:13, 16).

It is the exercise of biblical faith that materialism destroys. Like silt collecting on the bottom of a stream, the channel of faith becomes shallow. Faith loses it capacity to convey spiritual reality. The result is a faith of mere intellectual assent and dead orthodoxy.

In his book *The Last Battle* from The Chronicles of Narnia, C.S. Lewis suggests that the real battle of life is one of faith. In the last part of the book two groups of people, the dwarfs and the children, take refuge in an old barn from a raging battle. Both groups in the same building have two entirely different experiences. While the dwarfs see only a dark filthy barn, the children see a room filled with a warm bright light and a wonderful banquet.

The dwarfs could not see the banquet because during the battle for Narnia they had lost their ability to trust. They felt that they had seen too much deception and treachery. To protect themselves from future disappointment they had determined not to trust anymore. So, as far as their eyes could see, they had taken refuge in what was only a musty old barn.

The children too had seen deception. But they also had learned that Aslan, the Lion who ruled Narnia, was often near, even when they couldn't see him. When the battle looked like it was going to the enemies, the children had learned that somehow Aslan was in control.

Because they had faith the children were ready for the spiritual banquet before them. Their faith remained strong even when it had been difficult to believe. The banquet set before them was Aslan's reward. But the dwarfs, who lost faith, lost the privilege of Aslan's banquet.

Faith is a battle for us like it was for the dwarfs. With a faith made shallow by materialism we become blind to the spiritual life that God provides for his people. By faith we can see what others can't, and know what others don't. But with a shallow faith we see little, know little, and only end up with hay.

I feel sad when I hear the song "Material World." There is such emptiness in a life confined to a physical existence. I feel bad for those of us who have lost spiritual awareness. I don't want that for myself or for God's people. I want my life to be filled with his presence. I want a living faith, full of spiritual life that will allow me to be with God throughout my day. I want the study of God's Word to nourish my heart with spiritual truth. I want doctrines of the faith to be living guides that set my heart on fire.

How We See Materialism

Materialism wants me to believe:	"I am what I own."
How materialism is seen in the world:	Accumulation Affluence
How materialism is seen in the church:	Prosperity Apathy

How We Defeat Materialism

The biblical value to combat materialism:	Spirituality—"God's Spirit in me."
The spiritual discipline to combat materialism:	Meditation
The result of defeating materialism:	Faith

Figure 2. Defeating Materialism

An awareness of a spiritual reality alters forever the way we live and view the world. We understand that the quantity of our possessions does not make the quality of our lives. We see that preoccupation with an earthly existence can rob us of true spiritual experience. With spiritual strength we seek spiritual growth and spiritual maturity.

For Individuals or Groups

1. Reflect on the message of the Dragon of Materialism. In what ways does he suggest that our personal value is in what we own?

2. How does the Dragon of Materialism crowd out our awareness of the spiritual side of reality?

3. In what ways has the Dragon of Materialism invaded the church?

4. What are a few of the debilitating effects of materialism in our Christian experience?

5. How does the game of Monopoly illustrate one of the dangerous effects of materialism?

6. How does the lordship of Jesus Christ bring the physical and the

spiritual together? Why is it important to know this?

7. Reflect on your own experience of quiet time and meditation. In what ways can you identify with the type of quiet time that is focused on methods and techniques?

8. How can meditation and quiet time help us experience the spiritual?

9. Experience is an important part of a quiet time. What are some reasons why "experience" has been given a bad name?

10. Describe what you understand this statement to mean. "Materialism destroys the exercise of biblical faith."

11. How does the story about the spiritual banquet in *The Last Battle* illustrate the battle of faith?

3
The Dragon of Activism

A Responsive Peace
in a Busy Life

Every doubt I have about myself comes to the surface. Recently I was surrounded by Christian leaders at a national convention. I was overwhelmed at all they are doing and how effective they appeared. In comparison, my efforts seemed small. Initially I was tempted to talk big. But talking big didn't feel right. So I slipped off to my room to be alone.

In a day or two I knew that my insecurities would move back into place and a more healthy perspective would return. What others are doing will no longer sound so impressive and my work won't seem so small.

But something is wrong with the whole process. I shouldn't have responded like that. But I did. Deep inside I was convinced that my value was dependent on what I did and what I produced. "What do I have to show for my efforts?" I asked myself. I needed tangible results so I could say, "I have done this."

The Dragon of Activism had bitten me and its poison was in my blood. There is nothing wrong with hard work or wanting to be effective. The Scriptures encourage fruitful labor, and the church throughout history has taught the value of hard work. But activism is something more. It is a way of working that becomes a compulsion. Workaholics consumed with careers, mothers who push their children to achieve and students who are driven by the pursuit of good grades are all fueled by activism. In the wake of its path are stress-filled parents, burned-out pastors and broken relationships.

Activism arises from a deformed or, more correctly, a misplaced sense of responsibility. We have lost our sense of accountability to God and have put action and its results in his place. While some would see this shift as a liberation from the tyranny of a demanding God, we have simply placed ourselves under the tyranny of actions instead. Being responsible to God leaves room for grace, but the god of action and productivity is a merciless taskmaster. Even though we are always busy, he is never satisfied. We can never do enough.

Busyness

While I struggle with all the dragons, activism is one of my two personal pet dragons. I am constantly aware that there is always more to do in a day than there is time; and I feel compelled to do it all. There is a sense of urgency that never allows me to be content in one spot for long. The next place I am supposed to be or the next thing I am supposed to do is always exerting pressure. My life with God is a record of a continual struggle to escape this sense of being pushed from the inside.

Demands and opportunities come at us incessantly. Schoolchildren are kept busy with studies, sports and extracurricular activities. Parents have jobs, social responsibilities and family obligations. Meals together are increasingly rare. Family members greet each other coming and going.

From time to time in the midst of our busyness we sense that something is wrong. I was first confronted with my activism when we moved to Jackson. I was assigned there to direct campus ministry for two states—to me an overwhelming task. Determined to do the job, I set up an office in a back room of our house and was always rushing in and out the back door to the next appointment or meeting. Wayne, our next door neighbor, had a job with normal hours. While I was working long and hard, rushing in and out, he would watch me come and go, shaking his head at that busy Yankee.

Apart from a discussion or two at the back fence, Wayne and I had not really talked. So after living next to each other for a couple of months, Wayne decided that he would get to know me. As I went in and out, he would raise his big hand and holler at me to come over to his front porch for coffee. Now sitting on his front porch for coffee was the last thing I had time for. But it was impolite to refuse. So I would put a smile on my face and go sit down.

Initially I assumed a polite fifteen-minute conversation would be sufficient. Then I could excuse myself to get on with my business. But to my horror, I discovered that Wayne intended to talk for an hour or two! And he enjoyed talking so much that if I wasn't going to talk, then he would do the talking for both of us. After this happened a time or two I would try to look the other way as I went to and fro. But it didn't help. Wayne always gave a friendly call whenever he saw me, and then I knew that the next two hours were gone.

I didn't have time for this! I had great things to do. People were depending on me. There was a ministry to build. But over the next two years, I became thankful for his friendship. The little empire that I was planning to build for God didn't materialize to my satisfaction. I went through some dark times. When I was sure that God had deserted me, Wayne was there to encourage me. When I was feeling sorry for myself, Wayne was there to give me a kick in the pants.

This Dragon of Activism has captured many of us. Frequently we complain about busy schedules and lack of time. Yet few of us seem to be able to get our schedules under control—or even slow them down. It seems that our busyness is self-perpetuating. We are drawn into a cycle that feeds on itself. As our pace increases it becomes harder and harder to stop.

In one sense, it's fun to be busy, with lots to do. It makes us feel important. But the cost that we must pay for our busyness is high. Recently on a flight from Jackson to New Orleans, I sat next to an engineer for a national corporation. As we struck up a conversation he spoke of all the places his job takes him—to most of the fifty United States and to several countries overseas. (I wanted to talk about all my travels, but there was no way that I could match him.) The fact that he flew around so much said that he was very successful. But not only was he successful, his whole family was. He had a daughter who was a graduate of MIT, a son who was an executive for an a oil company and a wife who was the head of an insurance company. I was completely impressed!

But then the hitch. His wife lives in Boston while he lives in Jackson. He and his wife were so busy that something had to go. In their family it was intimate relationships.

Harry Chapin sang a song that captures the impact of activism on the family.

The cats in the cradle and the silver spoon;
Little boy blue and the man in the moon.
"When you coming home, Dad?" "Don't know when.

But we'll get together then.
Son, you know we'll have a good time then."
At the end of his life the father turns to his son, but by then
its too late. The refrain shifts:
"When you coming home, son?" "I don't know when.
But we'll get together then.
Dad, you know we'll have a good time then."

I Am What I Do

One of the reasons that we are driven to a life of busyness is that
our identity is tied up in what we do. When we meet someone,
the first or nearly the first question we ask is, "What do you do?"

Because we seek our value in what we do, we confuse ourselves
with our professions. When asked to identify ourselves we say,
"I am a doctor," or, "I am a teacher," or, "I am a plumber," or,
"I am a student." When we ask children what profession they are
going to choose when they grow up we ask, "What are you
going to *be?*"

While what we do is an important part of who we are, the
emphasis that we place on it is destructive. We become driven.
Personal value is not something I have, something intrinsic to
my being. Rather it is something I must achieve through my
actions. If I believe that my value comes from what I do (my job,
my accomplishments and so on), then I must give myself to them
completely.

The problem is, however, that the promise of self-worth never
materializes. We can never do enough. If we make an A in one
course, we must make it in the next. If we establish one company, we must establish another. If we win one race, we must
win the next. We can never say, "Now I have value. Now I am
significant." There is always one more thing we have to do.

In the Greek myth, Sisyphus was condemned by the gods to

push a huge stone up a hill. Just as he gets it to the top, it rolls down to the bottom and he has to push it back up again. And so on forever. Sisyphus was condemned to this task. The Dragon of Activism has tricked us into volunteering for it.

I Am What I Produce

According to activism, if something is going to happen in my world, it is up to me. Results (what I can produce) then become the only tangible means I can use to measure my value. If I have a lot to show for my effort, I have a great deal of value; if I have little to show for my efforts, then, I have little value.

Two of the words we use for results are *success* and *winning*. The highest compliment we can pay to someone is to say, "You're a winner!" or, "You're a success." In our pursuit of personal value there is little that we won't sacrifice to obtain this.

Every time I walk into a bookstore it seems there are several new titles on winning and success; as I scan the shelves I see *Winning through Intimidation, How to Develop a Winning Attitude, Success Is Yours, Eat to Win* and so on. Vince Lombardi, famous football coach of the Green Bay Packers, said, "Winning isn't everything. It's the only thing." While he was speaking of football, in an activistic culture, it applies to all areas of life. In sports it's points on the board; in business it's profit and expansion; in our personal lives, it's how much we possess or how well our children do. However we measure it, the issue is results.

Burnout is a word that has become common in our vocabulary in the past ten years. It describes a person who has lost all motivation to work, someone who is mentally and emotionally exhausted. Studies indicate that burnout happens not to those who work long hours but to those who set goals which they haven't been able to reach. In other words, they have not been able to produce the desired results! When we hang our personal value on results and then are continually unable to produce, deep disillusion and despair set in. Perhaps we have no value at all?

As you might have gathered from earlier remarks, I have gone through a period of burnout. As I went out to build the kingdom of God on college campuses, as I sought to organize students, as I looked for more staff, my ambitious plans were not met. Despite all the trust in God and the spiritual resources that I thought I had, one day I found myself in a pit of emotional and spiritual exhaustion—burnout.

I thought that burnout could only happen to business executives or worldly pastors of big churches. I thought that knowing about the Dragon of Activism was enough to deliver me. After all, I had lectured on it. But its grip on our minds—on my mind—was stronger than I had imagined. It is one thing to know about the Dragon of Activism, it is another thing to face it.

How to Do Everything

Activism not only requires action, it also requires a method. Once life is reduced to action and results, then all we have to do is discover the right procedure. At a management conference for Christians, I along with the dozens of others took temperament tests, personality tests and relational style tests. Once the testing was done, we started on the skills of management. When we were through with the week, we were supposed to know how to be effective ministers. I love this material. It appeals to my activism. I can take it back and produce a ministry that gets the results I want. The only problem is that that is precisely where I struggle with God.

It is all too easy for me to put my faith in method and effort, and not in God. The use of technique has worked well in science and industry, but even there it has its limitations. How much more does technique miss the mark when it is applied to other areas of life! Personal and spiritual matters don't lend themselves easily to technique. While methods can be helpful here, they can't guarantee results.

For most of life, there are too many variables which can't be reduced to a method. Parents can't make children turn out right. Doctors can't make a body heal. Farmers can't make a fruitful harvest. A stockbroker can't control the market. The painful reality is, we can't always accomplish our goals, no matter what technique we use. But that is precisely what the Dragon of Activism requires. If I can't get the results, then I don't have any value. And since activism won't always give results, the Dragon condemns me to perpetual failure even though it promises the opposite.

I suspect that the last straw prior to burnout is when people realize that hard work and right methods can't assure success.

Stress is another word that has taken on new significance in the past ten years. I believe the increasing role of technique bears a great deal of responsibility for this. While activism requires that we put our hope in technique, underneath that hope is a gnawing sense of doubt. What if there is not a "how to" that will work for my situation?

One corporate president observed that the word *fear* described most managers he knew over a thirty-year period. A study of several major corporations supports his impression. Managers were afraid that (a) they couldn't pull it off, (b) that they did not know enough, or (c) that there were events beyond their control that would eventually wreck their career.

Activism in the Church
You would think that the church would be free of activism. After all, don't we proclaim an all-powerful, all-loving God who we

can trust completely for our lives, our souls and our world? This should allow us to relax in him. But the reality is far from this.

Last spring everyone in our church seemed dry. The ministry opportunities which once looked great, now felt like burdens. Our Easter week activities were coming up, and I was in charge. Normally we have something going almost every night of the week. However, as I began preparation, I discovered that no one wanted to work on the planning committee. Furthermore, as I checked around I discovered that few people were even interested in coming to any Easter week activity!

About this same time we were holding elections for church officers. Eight of nine people asked refused to accept nominations. Such behavior was out of character. Our church is small, but it is made up of highly committed members who join because of the opportunity for all to be involved in ministry. As a church we were experiencing burnout.

Bill, our pastor, called a congregational meeting to discuss the situation. We concluded that while we were busy doing things in the name of Christ, somewhere we had shifted from a focus on God to a focus on our activities. With good intentions we had assumed tasks because we thought we were being obedient to the gospel. But the ministries themselves were now the center; God had been moved into a secondary position. At some point the demands we were living under had to bring us to exhaustion. They did.

Powerless, frustrated and overworked, churches are full of tired Christians. Our church experienced what many others do as well. Fortunately, our pastor had the perception to see the real problem and do something about it. But the Dragon of Activism blinds so that many don't see the way out. Frequently the approach to overcoming unfruitful ministry and burnout is to try new programs and new activities.

Activism makes service, not God, the goal of the Christian life. Mature Christians are seen as those who are busy doing things for God. The best churches are the ones that offer the most programs and activities. Every night of the week there are opportunities for Bible study, choir, aerobic exercise, visitation, supper clubs, scouting, sports and a thousand other things.

In the early years of my Christian life I used to cry out repeatedly for God to use me. And he did. Gradually, however, I discovered that a major reason why I want God to use me is that I am unsure of his love. So I hope my service will indicate my worth to him. When ministry does not go according to my plans, then I begin to wonder if God really loves me.

We may believe that we are giving our lives in service to God when we are only serving the Dragon of Activism. Businessmen have consuming careers; pastors and Christian workers have consuming ministries. Family and personal needs go unfulfilled in the misguided belief that God calls us to busyness.

Congregations evaluate a pastor's worth by how busy he is, how many new members he has brought in and how many new programs he has introduced. Pastors' offices which used to be places of study and prayer are today administrative nerve centers of Christian conglomerates.

Like the world, we too put our faith in technique. Our church is not growing? There is a ready-made program that will bring results. Want to do evangelism? There is a technique you can learn in five easy steps. Maybe discipleship is what our fellowship needs? The twelve essential principles have been distilled from Scripture; so just buy the right book and follow directions.

Our faith in technique shouts from the shelves of Christian bookstores. "How to" books are everywhere: *How to Be a Disciple, How to Win Your Friends to Christ, How to Study the Bible, How to Be Spiritually Fit.* . . .

But once the church is larger, once the converts are in, we are at a loss for what to do next except start another program. Where is the experience of divine fellowship that should characterize the church? Where is God in all this? God is reduced from the One we worship to the one who helps us do our ministries.

How do we escape? First by discovering that our activistic service for God is only another expression of worldliness. We need God, not more ministries. We need the power of the Spirit, not more programs. We need to find out what it really means to serve God.

Biblical Responsibility

The Dragon of Activism dies a quiet death when I understand what true responsibility is. I know freedom when I know God as my Lord.

The urgency that pushes me from the inside is relieved when I shift my focus from actions and results to God. Even as I write there is an anxiety to finish this chapter. I've got to get it done. I pause to remind myself that God wants my faithful obedience, not "profound thoughts" in a book. And when in my heart I submit to God, in the place of the tyranny of the urgent, I know deep peace and a quiet settled order.

This doesn't always happen immediately or all at once. I take small steps forward, hit a snag and go backward, and move ahead again on my trek toward a deep calm before God. But there is progress as my mind clears and I see God as the Lord of creation to whom I am responsible. Our first parents were made stewards of God's world, responsible to tend and keep it. They named the animals and cultivated the ground. We inherit their stewardship, bent as it may have been by the Fall.

Created responsible, I am to be a responder. God is the Lord of his world and has not relinquished control of it nor abandoned it. The work I do is in response to his work. My efforts are limited both by the abilities he gives me and the tasks to which he calls me.

When I am responsive to God, I am not driven, not consumed by my goals and actions. The next meeting I am supposed to be at does not pull at me in the same way. I am more in control of my actions, not controlled by them. At such times I am also less tempted to value myself and others by productivity. When I am responsive to God, I am free to be productive or just to be faithful. I am free to use methods without being subject to them.

This radical responsiveness affects every area of life. Results don't come because of human effort or skill but from the Lord. The Psalmist acknowledges, "I do not trust in my bow, my sword does not bring me victory; but you give us victory over our enemies" (Ps 44:6-7). I like to take credit when things turn out right. But God wants me to know that my efforts are fruitless on my own.

As God prepared Israel to take the Promised Land, he warned them not to confuse the coming prosperity with their own efforts. "You may say to yourself, 'My power and the strength of my hands have produced this wealth for me.' But remember the LORD your God, for it is he who gives you the ability to produce wealth" (Deut 8:17-18). Here there is no room for activism. God is the Lord of Israel, providing for them and blessing their efforts.

It is the same for us. Despite what the Dragon of Activism tells us, God brings results. Whether in my studies or my family or my business, God determines the outcome. "In his heart a man plans his course, but the LORD determines his steps" (Prov 16:9).

Not long ago my next door neighbor, Wayne, left his job and is now finishing college with plans to attend seminary next year. Eventually he hopes to enter some type of ministry. I'm not claiming the credit, but our porch conversations were a significant factor as God led him in this way. I had no idea that as God was teaching me to be responsive, he was also working in Wayne. But that is what being responsive is all about. God sets the agenda and while in the end it may not be the same as mine, he brings blessings.

Christians before us have understood this clearly. About three hundred years ago Cotton Mather, the American Puritan wrote, "At no time of day may we expect that our business will succeed without God's blessing. . . . All fall out as God shall order it."[1] And Martin Luther wrote, "When riches come, the godless heart of man thinks, 'I have achieved this with my labors.' It does not consider that they are purely blessing of God, blessing that at time come to us through our labors and at time without our labors, but never because of our labors: for God always gives them because of his undeserved mercy."[2]

While we are dependent on our Lord, I am not suggesting that we are just tagging along in some meaningless manner. The opposite of activism is not passivism. Nor is biblical responsibility actually determinism in disguise. We are significant, and so are the abilities and tasks that God has given us. We must live in the balance—responsibility—where there is freedom and challenge.

David was able to take on Goliath because he knew that the outcome did not depend on numbers or weapons. Gideon, one of my favorite characters of Scripture, was called to lead an army. He had no training as a soldier, was not known for his courage and was sent against thousands with just three hundred men. The Scriptures are full of people who took on jobs that were too

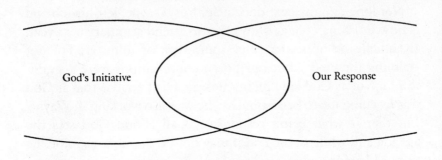

Figure 3. God's Initiative and Our Response

big. When we know that the battle is the Lord's we can confidently wade into tasks for which we feel incapable.

But we are not confident of results. We are confident in God. A responsiveness to God does not guarantee success—at least not as you and I are accustomed to defining it. Jeremiah was called to be a prophet to a people who would not listen to him. Jesus was sent to a people who rejected and killed him. Many of the heroes of faith listed in Hebrew 11 are people who were not successful in worldly terms.

Biblical responsibility means that I am free to fail and still not be a failure. The central question I have to ask myself is, "Am I doing what I am supposed to do to the best of my abilities?" The rest rests with God. There is no need to prove my worth. I am created in his image. My worth is not dependent on what I do or produce, but on him whom I obey. Success is not my goal. The issue is responsiveness. Nothing I do has any lasting significance or meaning apart from his personal involvement and blessing.

Prayer
The one thing that strikes at the heart of our activism is prayer.

In prayer God is placed back in the center of our lives as the One who determines who we are and what do.

Prayer is difficult, even for a recovering activist such as myself. When we believe that we can accomplish our goals by our own effort there is little desire to pray. Jacques Ellul observes, "The man of our time does not know how to pray; but much more than that, he has neither the desire nor the need to do so."[3]

I must constantly remind myself to pray. More frequently than I care to admit, I am at the end of a decision-making process before I remember that I haven't consulted the Lord. "Oh, yeah, I better pray about that." Despite my good intentions there is always one more phone call, one more page to read, one more person to see. Somehow the time set aside for prayer for this day, this week, this year, slips between the cracks of my busy schedule. Ellul observes, "To pray goes against the natural bent that I instinctively am because inclined that way by my culture, my surrounding, and my work. There is already a combat here, at the most humble level."[4]

The extent of our lack of prayer betrays how much activism controls us. Prayer is not even a central part of most church life. The midweek prayer meetings, for churches that have them, are just one more service where there is singing and preaching. And if there is an hour set aside to pray, the majority of time will be spent talking and rehearsing requests. Usually, only in the last ten or fifteen minutes do we actually get around to prayer.

Even when we do pray, how our prayers are infected by activism! We offer up to God a shopping list of things which we think he should do. Or we ask his guidance and strength for the things that we are doing for him.

The place to begin in prayer is to confess that we don't pray enough and that we don't pray well. I was greatly helped by a simple statement by Richard Foster in *Celebration of Discipline*.

"One of the liberating experiences of my life came when I understood that prayer involved a learning process."[5]

Another revolutionary insight about prayer for me has been the discovery that prayer is a dialog not a monolog. In prayer God speaks to us and we respond to him. Throughout Scripture, prayer is a dialog with God that precedes and guides all action. God spoke to Abraham, calling him to the Promised Land. Abraham's prayers were responses to God's actions and promises. God spoke to Moses and called him to guide Israel. Moses' life was a dialog with God about Israel. And so it is throughout the Scripture with David, the Prophets and the Apostles.

Hearing God speak is not something just for the mystic who lives in the desert or just for those in "Bible times." In *Daring to Draw Near*, John White writes, "God is always speaking. To hear his voice is not usually a mystical experience. . . . To hear him involves not so much a tuning into the right frequency as much as a humble recognition that it is his prerogative to speak and our responsibility to respond."[6] Luther wrote, "I do not know it and do not understand it, but sounding from above and ringing in my ears I hear what is beyond the thought of Man."[7]

Since prayer is a dialog, we need to learn to listen. In listening prayer we cultivate a sense of quiet in our hearts in which there is a space for God to speak. As I sit silently in prayer I find a hunger that wells up from inside and pulls me into a deep sense of communion with him.

I have a long way to go. I find encouragement from Psalm 32:8-9. "I will instruct you and teach you in the way you should go; I will counsel you and watch over you. Do not be like the horse or the mule, which have no understanding but must be controlled by bit and bridle or they will not come to you." In listening prayer I find that I am in a responsive state in which my plans are set aside. I look to him to set my agenda and guide me.

Because prayer is a dialog, I can look to God to teach me to pray. Andrew Murray in *The Ministry of Intercession* writes, "Be quiet before God and give him an opportunity; in due season you will learn to pray."[8]

Peace

The demands to be busy will not go away. I have obligations to my children that require time at school plays and soccer practices. I have commitments to my church that involve me on committees and special projects. I have a job that requires appointments with people, evening meetings and time on the road. And with all the activity, I am expected to produce results. So how am I supposed to face these responsibilities without succumbing to the Dragon?

One of my favorite Hebrew words is *shalom*. It is a broad word, rich in meaning. It is used to describe all of life being brought together in a harmonious whole.

During the early years of my Christian life I used to walk on the shore of the Gulf of Mexico at sunset. As I watched the huge red ball of the sun sink into the water, listened to the waves crashing on the sand, felt the wind blowing across the water, saw the clouds perform a light show of colors—in it all, I knew a sense of peace that went beyond words, a peace that passed understanding. Everything fit together in a cosmic harmony. I was drawn into worship as I knew that the Person who made it all was my Lord who knew my name. That for me describes shalom.

Shalom or peace is what God brings to his responsive people. Shalom is the ultimate blessing that God promises to Israel when he comes to redeem them and rule over them. To proclaim peace is to proclaim, "Your God reigns" (Is 52:7). When Jesus greets the disciples after the resurrection, his first word is,

How We See Activism

Activism wants me to believe:	"I am what I do." "I am what I produce."
How activism is seen in the world:	Consuming careers
How activism is seen in the church:	Consuming ministry

How We Defeat Activism

The biblical value to combat activism:	Responsibility—"God makes me fruitful."
The spiritual discipline to combat activism:	Dialogical prayer
The result of defeating activism	Peace

Figure 4. Defeating Activism

"Peace." He is not talking about a nice feeling, but about sha-lom, the blessing of life brought into order under his lordship.

To be under the sway of the Dragon of Activism is to be eccentric, to be off center. Like an imbalanced wheel that spins and wobbles until it breaks apart, so a life of activism can't hold together. With Christ at the center of my life I may still spin, but in a balanced way. I won't break off in a thousand different directions at once.

I don't need the beach to know that sense of deep peace. I can find it in a restful time of listening prayer. After my painful and embarrassing experience of burnout, I took seriously the abso-lute necessity of practicing responsiveness. I seek to be faithful in following his commands while leaving the results to him. I don't want to be driven by the Dragon of Activism. I don't want to measure my worth by what I do and produce.

There is a peace of God that will guard our hearts (Phil 4:7). In him is a focus that brings order and a settled pace to life.

For Individuals or Groups

1. Activism is a misplaced sense of responsibility. What is the danger that comes from believing we are responsible for results rather than being responsible to God?

2. The four marks of activism are (a) busyness, (b) finding our significance in what we do and (c) what we produce, and (d) a faith in technique. In what ways do you see these in your life? Give examples.

3. Why are techniques and methods insufficient to produce the results that we so strongly desire?

4. Describe the relationship first between burnout and activism, and then between stress and activism.

5. What are some of the marks of a church infected by activism?

6. How does a clear grasp of the lordship of Christ strike at the heart of activism?

7. How does a proper grasp of biblical responsibility free us to fail in a task we may undertake without feeling that we are personal failures?

8. In what ways does prayer help us to live with a proper sense of responsibility?

9. What is the difference between prayers that are infected by activism and prayers that are responsive to God?

10. Christian prayer is a dialog not a monolog. What struggle might you face as you seek to listen in prayer rather than to do all the talking?

11. The result of a responsive life is shalom. In your own words define shalom.

12. What are some changes you might consider in the way you live after facing the Dragon of Activism?

4
The Dragon of Individualism

Personal Intimacy in a Lonely World

Jesus—yes!"
"The church—no!"

I saw the phrase on a sign held up high in a student demonstration several years ago in a display of anger at the church. The feelings about the church run deeply. Bring up the subject in any group and immediately you get a response. Some are for it. Many are against it. But everyone has a strong opinion.

Interestingly, at least to me, is the amount of negative feelings I discover in people I consider committed Christians. Just this past week I had lunch with a businessman who had just stopped attending a Monday morning prayer meeting at his church—a meeting he had been a part of for five years. Don put down his fork, leaned across the table and in an expression of quiet anger and said, "It's the same superficial stuff every week—stiff prayers and shallow sharing. It's always 'Pray for Aunt Martha's toe,' or, 'Pray for my friend to come to church.' People never really talk about what's going on inside them!"

The anger runs deep because our expectations run high. We have a hunger for spiritual relationships, not only with God, but with each other. We expect the church to be a place where we can know others and can be known by others. Everyone, Christian and non-Christian, expects the church to be a place where we are cared for. And yet it is a place filled with passiveness, a place where people go on Sunday mornings, shake hands, say, "How do you do? I'm fine," and leave.

There are churches where people drink deeply from each other. "How are you?" elicits a sharing of the heart to a listening ear. I know because I have been in some. But there are too many churches where intimacy among people does not exist. And even within churches where some special care is going on among people, there are those who seem to sit on the sidelines, longing to get in but never quite being able to move in.

I find a Dragon at work here, the Dragon of Individualism. His creed is, "I am the source of my own value." Firmly seated in our minds he locks us inside ourselves and locks others out.

Rugged individualists—that's how we like to perceive ourselves—independent and full of initiative. John Wayne and Lee Iacocca are our heroes. Certainly, encouraging a strong sense of individuality has produced great benefits for us. But our sense of individuality easily becomes an individualism, and we become self-centered as a way of life. It is apparent that we are currently embarked on a cultural preoccupation with self. The students of the seventies were characterized as the Me Generation. But preoccupation with self is not limited to the campus or the seventies. We have become the Me Culture.

It should not be surprising that we are preoccupied with self. The loss of the spiritual dimension to our lives reduces people to bodies with nothing inside. "Who am I?" becomes a burning question. And if there are no spiritual resources to draw on or share with others, then we are left alone with ourselves. If matter is all that matters and action and technique are the way to success, then I must find the resources to achieve value within myself. I am the key.

Even while seeking to know one another, we face each other through the filter of this Dragon. We can't reach others even when we try. Broken commitments, an inner uncertainty and a prevailing sense of isolation are the results.

How can we know and be known? How can we be the church as we sense it ought to be? We must recover the relational dynamic of knowing God that we all hunger for. Yet, until we are aware of the work of the Dragon of Individualism, we will be discontent with ourselves and the church and never know why.

I Am Looking for Me

The Dragon of Individualism proclaims a selfishness without guilt. Robert Ringer propagates the gospel of individualism in his book *Looking Out For Number One*. He writes, "Our primary objective is really to be as happy as possible and all other objectives great and small are only a means to that end."[1] He may say it a little too blatantly for our comfort, but he writes what we all believe. The greatest satisfaction and pleasure in life is for those who focus on themselves.

I'm not sure, however, that self-preoccupation is everything it is supposed to be. I remember being painfully self-conscious as a teen-ager. I struggled to discover how all that I was fit together so I could choose a direction in life. What about my interest in music? Should I devote myself to that? But how far can one go in life playing guitar and drums? And did I really have the talent? And how about my interest in reading? Would that lead to an academic career? Probably not since I spent a great deal of time escaping into science fiction but not much time studying.

Those were important questions. How I answered them would determine a great deal about my life. But they were hard questions, full of struggle.

The current focus on self extends beyond the teen years into a kind of perpetual adolescence. The choice of a career, the starting of a family, buying a house—things that were supposed to mean a sense of established identity didn't seem to provide that. So who I am is never really settled.

"Looking out for number one" quickly becomes a "looking for me." We are always on a journey into ourselves. Shirley Mac-Laine writes, "When you look back on your life and try to figure out where you've been and where you are going . . . what you find out is that the person you really go to bed with is yourself. The only thing you have is working to the consummation of your own identity."[2]

Unlimited Me

In the interest of pursuing me, the Dragon of Individualism proclaims personal liberation, freedom from limits. The only way that I can discover me, is to be free to be me. Nothing must hinder my individuality.

The authors of the book, *Habits of the Heart*, which deals with the current emphasis on individualism in America write, "Freedom is . . . a deeply held American value . . . in both personal and political life. Yet freedom turns out to mean being left alone by others, not have other people's values, ideas, or styles of life forced upon one."[3]

Words such as *restraint* and *self-discipline* belong to an outdated period of history. Now limits are considered unnecessary and unhealthy. We don't want our children to be inhibited, after all.

In more extreme forms this unlimited individuality may be seen in trends toward androgeny. More commonly it may just be an attitude of self-centeredness that permeates my life. Whatever the issue, I must be free. All outside limits are unwelcome infringements.

Liberated individualism destroys the bonds that have been built between people. Relationships are for my benefit and my first obligation is always to myself; commitments are commitments of convenience.

I was struck by this in the movie *Kramer vs. Kramer.* In it we see the painful struggle of a father and a son to rebuild their lives when the mother leaves to "find herself." While painful for everyone, her departure is considered acceptable. The irony was that while the movie was being made, one of the actors was going through a divorce.

Sadly, the movie reflects reality. For the past decade we have seen a large divorce rate, almost fifty per cent. People are willing to terminate a marriage if it is perceived as a restraint on personal growth and happiness. There is no sense of life-long obligation.

All areas of social life break apart in the name of liberated individuality. Children grow to ignore the limits of family obligations. Social concern for needs of others or issues that affect our society as a whole go unnoticed unless they directly affect me. I feel no responsibility.

Lonely Me

Individualism becomes a way of life that is habitually and naturally exclusive. The authors of *Habits of the Heart* observe "Even bonds of marriage and parenthood don't overcome the isolation that is ultimately the lot of each individual."[4] Preoccupation with me leaves me with me. My wants, my goals and my desires are the only things that matter. Is it any wonder that loneliness becomes a way of life? I hear it on the radio. I see it in movies and on TV. On the way to the airport this morning I heard an old song by Neil Diamond. The refrain says it all, " 'I am,' I said. 'I am,' I cried. And no one heard at all, not even the chair."[5]

Self-centered devotion leaves little time to know others or to be known by others. Narcissus, the handsome youth in the Greek myth, was enamored with his appearance. He only had eyes for himself and gazed at his reflection in a pool. As individualists we see only ourselves in the reflection of others. Even when we speak of needing to experience love and intimacy it is for the purpose of self-fulfillment, not because we care for another.

The loneliness of individualism is not just any kind of loneliness. It is a suffocating loneliness. It is a deep-in-your-bones loneliness, and you can't get it out. It is loneliness in the midst of a crowd. It is loneliness when you are on a date. It is loneliness when you are with your wife and family. It is loneliness wherever you go and whatever you do.

The irony is that we are lonely and we don't know why.

An Individualistic Church

Because of the Dragon of Individualism, being discipled, church membership and knowing God are all lost. Any aspect of our faith that connects us with others fades away. As the Dragon works his spell, the gospel is reoriented away from God toward me. Tentative commitments to the church result in a casual participation, and loneliness inside the church becomes a way of life.

One expression of individualism in the church is the gospel of self-esteem and self-fulfillment. The message is that faith in Christ makes us feel good about ourselves.

There is some truth here. The leper Jesus healed certainly felt better about himself. So did the paralytic that carried his bed away. But a gospel of self-esteem comes perilously close to turning Christianity on its head. Classical Christianity begins with the character of God, his attributes and his standards. The first question in the Westminster catachism is, "What is the chief end of man?" with the answer, "To glorify God and enjoy him forever." But once individualism settles in, the holiness of God becomes a vague idea. We don't even realize that we are no longer asking what the unlimited God requires. Instead we think of him as the One who can satisfy me. The Twenty-third Psalm could be rephrased from, "The Lord is my shepherd, I shall not want," to "The Lord is my shepherd, he gives me everything I want."

A. W. Tozer wrote, "What comes into our minds when we think about God is the most important thing about us."[6] To shift the phrase a bit, if the Dragon of Individualism gets a hold of us, then the most important thing about God is how God makes me feel about me.

In the spiritual classics there is a strikingly different attitude toward self. They emphasized humility and self-denial. Thomas à Kempis in *The Imitation of Christ* writes, "But if I abase myself and . . . shrink from all self-esteem . . . Thy grace will be favorable to me, and Thy light near unto my heart."[7]

À Kempis knows what we seem to miss. It is difficult to escape from ourselves, and until we do, we never enjoy God. We become so full of ourselves that there is no place for God. If we believe that we have a divine sanction for a life devoted to me, how will we ever be turned from ourselves to have the privilege of knowing God?

When we are beguiled by the Dragon of Individualism, it is hard to make the commitment necessary for the church to be a nourishing community. We slip into making commitments of convenience.

Once when I was asked to give a talk on commitment at Georgia Tech, I tried an experiment. At the beginning of the talk I passed out a card and asked the students to make a formal commitment to membership in their campus fellowship. There was a stony silence in the room. Only a couple of people were willing to sign. Most looked at me suspiciously. After a minute or two I explained that this was only an illustration to introduce my talk. There was relieved but uncomfortable laughter around the room.

As church members we hardly realize that such commitments are even necessary. Since we think so much in terms of our own agenda, there is little experience of corporate life.

At a weekend conference last spring, this became painfully evident. The conference was to start on Friday night and go until Sunday afternoon. It was to be a time to learn from an able Bible teacher and to develop better friendships. But starting Saturday morning students began coming to me to explain why they had to leave early. First one, then another. A test on Monday, a date Saturday night and so on. By Sunday morning almost half our conference had disappeared! No one intended to wreck it, but that is almost what happened. Friendships were begun but never established. Those who stayed until the end felt something was missing.

Individualism has its effect on churches too. When people have low commitment, it becomes easier to move from church to church. Either we are upset with some aspect of church life or we really like the new preacher down the road. Thus our individualism leaves us lonely inside the church as well as outside the church.

Taming the Dragon of Individualism

Relationships are at the heart of the church. And relationships are at the foundation of our sense of identity. But when we turn to the Scriptures there is a relational, a corporate side to life that we miss because we read Scripture with "individualized" eyes.

God is the great Self, the I AM. The Father, Son and Spirit, each person of the Godhead in relationship to the other. And so we, made in his image, male and female, are also selves in relationship.

In view of the relational nature of God and of people, it is not surprising that the theme of relationship runs throughout the Old Testament and New Testament. We must pay attention to it if we are to escape the Dragon of Individualism.

There is a priority on peoplehood in the Old Testament. Knowing God and personal identity were corporate concepts. God's offer of salvation is corporate, "I will be your God and you will be my people." Even the outstanding individuals that we know about in the Old Testament are known because of the role of the people—Abraham, Isaac and Jacob as the fathers of the people; Moses as the deliverer of the people; Joshua and Gideon as generals of the people; David and Solomon as kings of the people; and so on.

This corporate concept of life became an integral part of Hebrew thought. Personal blessing sought from God has a corporate perspective. The Psalmist cries out for the blessing of God, "Remember me, O LORD, when you show favor to your people, come to my aid when you save them, that I may enjoy the prosperity of your chosen ones, that I may share in the joy of your nation and join your inheritance in giving praise" (Ps 106:4-5). He knew that his own personal welfare was conditional upon the welfare of the entire nation.

Sin was part of Israel's collective consciousness as well as blessing. When Daniel confesses the sin of the nation and seeks forgiveness, he prays, "O Lord, the great and awesome God, who keeps his covenant of love with all who love him and obey his commands, we have sinned and done wrong . . ." (Dan 9:4-5). The actual sins he confessed were never ones he personally committed. In fact they had been committed before he was born!

The same corporate theme is in the New Testament. Salvation, we find, is corporate. When the angel appears to Joseph, he says that Jesus will "save his people from their sins" (Mt 1:21). There is a corporate focus to Jesus' ministry. He calls twelve disciples and trains them as a group for the purpose of establishing a church while teaching them to pray "Our Father in heaven, . . ." and telling them that when two or three pray, "there I am in your midst."

The apostle Paul admonishes the Philippians to work out their salvation in fear and trembling, for "God works among you to accomplish his purpose" (Phil 2:13). And when he prays for the Ephesians, he asks that they "may have power, together with all the saints, to grasp how wide and long and high and deep is the love of Christ" (Eph 3:18).

Peter calls on every corporate word he can think of when he writes, "You are a chosen people, a royal priesthood, a holy nation, a people belonging to God, . . . Once you were not a people, but now you are the people of God" (1 Pet 2:9-10).

Uniquely Me

The corporate element of our identity does not mean that we are lost in a sea of others, somehow merged into a collective whole. God is the God who knows each of us by name. We are each formed in the womb with days that are planned before we are born. We all have a unique function in the world that only we can fill.

While the Old Testament has a corporate emphasis, it also has an individual one as well. God had personal relationships with individuals. Whether it was an outstanding leader like Moses, a colorful character like Gideon or a widow near starvation to whom God sent Elijah, God cared for people on an individual basis. The prophets were outstanding individuals in the nation. Standing with Israel, they also were separate from her, calling for repentance. John the Baptist, as the last of the Old Testament prophets, illustrates their role; living in the desert alone, he calls the people out to repent.

I am always impressed with the sense of individuality of the apostle Paul whenever I read his epistles. While he is committed to the building of the church, his strong personality and determined will are on every page he writes. I once counted nine references to himself in three verses!

It is the balance of individuals in relationship that form an adequate identity. It is the dynamic balance which creates a healthy individuality. If I move to either extreme, I lose a healthy sense of self. If I am preoccupied with me, eventually I feel insignificant, isolated and confused about who I am. On the other hand, if I am completely immersed in others, I lose my sense of uniqueness and also feel insignificant and confused about my identity.

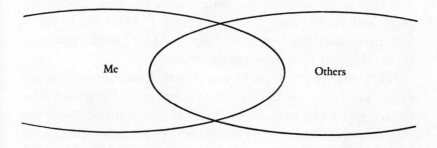

Figure 5. The Balance of Identity

The Discipline of Community

The church is more than just a collection of saved souls. But we must practice the discipline of community if we are to tame the Dragon of Individualism. We need to gain a proper sense of our own identity and understand what it means to be a part of the people of God.

In Jesus' command, "Love one another as I have loved you," I find the starting point for the practice of community. More than a feeling, the love of Jesus is a selecting choice. I used to picture the church as a large meeting room with thousands of people and a speaker so far away that I could hardly see him. I felt like a faceless unknown at the edge of the crowd, unknown to the speaker or anyone else.

But such an image is wrong. I may be in a room, so to speak, with thousands of people, all who have come to learn from the speaker, but I am in the room because I have been personally invited in by the One at the front. "You have not chosen me, but I have chosen you."

In the same way, the practice of community is choosing one another as God chose us. That's what Jesus' command to love each other means. We are all in the same room because Jesus has chosen us and brought us in. He is what we all have in common. But that is not enough for community. We look around the room and think, "Now there is a person I would like to know, and maybe him. But look at that guy, and her! I hope I can avoid them. Maybe if I just look the other way. . . ."

While that is going on in our minds, Jesus turns to us and says, "Love one another as I have loved you." That is, I have chosen you to be part of me, to be at one with me. Now you turn to each other, all of you, and choose each other in the same way. So now in Christian community, we not only face forward, but we turn and face each other as well. The basis of our choice is not the likability of another, but the expectation of our Lord.

The practice of Christian community is a struggle. Some of the deepest hurts I ever received have come from believers with whom I had shared a great deal. But the issue is not whether I benefit or not. We have been made a part of God's people by our submission to Christ. We must not think of ourselves as separate, whether it is convenient or inconvenient, whether it is painful or pleasurable.

Problems seem to be a normal part of being in God's people. This should not be surprising since the church is where needy people come together. It wasn't long before the New Testament believers had to face the problem of discrimination in the food distribution between Greek Jews and Palestinian Jews, the lie of Ananias and Sapphira, what to do with the zealous convert, Saul of Tarsus, the conversion of the Gentiles and many other issues. But it is in struggles like these that God is shaping and molding us to be who he intends us to be.

The corporate sense of knowing God, the sense of people-hood that is in the Scriptures will not naturally develop just because we are getting together with a few people. Our Dragon of Individualism will keep walls up so that we maintain our distance. We must choose to drop our own walls and choose to get past the walls of others.

The practice of community is a choice that requires commitment. We must choose to do it and to keep at it. We do it because we are supposed to, not just because it works. We choose each other because our Lord commanded us to follow his example. So we do, day after day after day.

I have found that small groups are ideal for practicing community. Meeting regularly with the same people to share and do Bible study has been a wonderful tool to aid in the corporate experience of knowing God.

There is vitality in a group of people who are experiencing Christian community. The book of Acts and the epistles of the New Testament are charged with a sense of electricity. People were together in the name of Christ, and they enjoyed it. The pleasure of community is *in participating, in sharing, in belonging* and *in being together.*

First, the vitality of community is the pleasure of *participation.* Energy is produced when we sense that we are a part of something that is bigger than we are. As the apostles preached, taught and healed, the entire church was filled with joy. Jesus was present in his church and everyone felt privileged to be a part of it. Members of sports teams and armies taste some of the pleasure of this on a limited scale. How much better it is to participate in the community of the king where we all belong.

We may not all have a leading role as Christians, yet we are never passive observers. We can never say, "I'm not important here," and slip into an apathetic distance from others. Soon after Pentecost, the apostles began to distribute responsibility, first to the seven deacons and then others. By the time we get into the epistles there are lists of gifts and responsibilities, and we are all urged to use our talents for the good of each other.

Second, in Christian community there is pleasure in *sharing.* As I discuss my pains and pleasure of the week with fellow believers in my small group I have a sense of being understood. Here are others who share my values. And often, the things that upset me, upset them. The struggles that I face are similar to the struggles that they face. And, of course, it is a two-way street. When I offer understanding to them, I find satisfaction in having provided a helping hand.

Third, in community there is pleasure in *belonging.* It is nourishing to know that you are a part of a group of people who know you and care for you. People know when you are there and miss you when you aren't. Although I am often out of town for our small group or Sunday meetings, I'm always glad that one or two will come up to me and say, "We are glad you are here. We missed you last week."

Fourth, there is pleasure in just being together. I find it most nourishing because I don't always have to do something productive. I find a spiritual and even mystical interaction in the normal, mundane routines of the church. In gatherings of fellow believers, around the picnic table or the coffee urn with friends who know me, I discover that while God may not be mentioned by name I often walk away thinking of the goodness of God and I know that I have been in his presence.

Intimacy

What is it like to be a member of God's family? For me it is like being lost, wandering around on a cold winter night with the temperature below zero and snow swirling around me. My food is gone and I am too weak to go on much farther. But as I was about to give up hope I walk over a hill, and in the distance I see a small light. I make my way as best I can to the cabin, knock on the door desperately and collapse when someone opens it. I am startled to see several of my dearest friends inside. They take off my frozen clothes, wrap me in a huge warm bearskin, set up a chair next to the roaring fire and put a steaming mug in my hands. After I recover, we sit together talking, laughing and reading (from C. S. Lewis) for hours. I expect that heaven will be something like this, safe and warm after the danger of the cold, being with people I love and who love me.

There is pleasure beyond words in knowing and being known. It is something spiritual—spirit relating to spirit. The church, more than any other place can be the place where such intimacy is experienced.

How We See Individualism

Individualism wants me to believe:	"I am the source of my own value."
How individualism is seen in the world:	Liberated loneliness
How individualism is seen in the church:	Christian loneliness

How We Defeat Individualism

The biblical value to combat individualism:	Relationships—"God made us in his image."
The spiritual discipline to combat individualism:	Community
The result of defeating individualism:	Intimacy

Figure 6. Defeating Individualism

But this intimacy is not a romantic ideal. It is reality. In the church, what we have to give to each other is our hurts and pains. The church is to be a safe place and a healing place because we are all in this together.

Our small group took a retreat together a month ago. We arranged baby sitters for the kids, rearranged work schedules and went off together to spend a couple of days in the mountains of Arkansas. It was an intimate time for Jan and Allen, Hervey and Theresa, and Jackie and I—three couples in a small cabin. As we talked together, ate together and cleaned together the relational cracks began to come out.

"Why do you always appear to have it together. Why don't you share your hurts?"

"Why haven't you shown any interest in getting together outside of the group's meetings?"

"Why aren't you interested in my writing?"

And we shared high points.

"I didn't know you thought I could teach well. I've never thought of myself that way before!"

"What do you mean I have a gentle spirit?"

By the time our retreat was over, I was ready to go home. I knew more about some people than I wanted to know before the weekend. I had shown more of myself than I had wanted to show. But something happened to us all. A deeper trust perhaps. We know in deeper ways that there is acceptance of one another.

We have chosen to go on together.

For Individuals or Groups

1. Most of us have had good and bad experiences in the church. Are there times when you have struggled with loneliness and isolation in your church experience? Explain.

2. The loss of the spiritual dimension of life has contributed to the current preoccupation with self. Explain how this is so.

3. What are some of the ways the individualistic call for personal liberation from all restraints has affected our world?

4. In what ways do you see the loneliness created by individualism expressed in the media, the movies, in music and among people that you know?

5. How can the gospel of self-esteem and self-fulfillment be a dangerous departure from classical Christianity?

6. In what ways does individualism affect our participation in the life of the church?

7. Why does it take the balance of relationships and a sense of individuality to form a healthy sense of identity?

8. Love is both a desire and discipline which strikes at the heart of the Dragon of Individualism. Explain how love as a choice is the foundation of Christian community.

9. While community is a discipline, it is also a pleasure. How have you tasted the pleasures of Christian community?

10. When we have made our way past the Dragon of Individualism, we can expect to taste the experience of intimacy. How then do you

respond to the following statement: "In the church what we have to give to each other is our hurts and pains"?

11. Have you ever had the privilege of sharing hurts and pains in a group of believers? What was it like?

5
The Dragon of Conformism

Contentment with Ourselves and God

The Dragon of Individualism has a traveling companion—conformism.

As we saw in the last chapter, the church is to be a priority for us. The mystery of biblical faith is that we know God together. The Dragon of Individualism tries to prevent us from enjoying this great reality. But even after we have tamed him, the struggle is not over. There is another Dragon that must be tamed as well—the Dragon of Conformism. Until he is faced we will continue to be angry and frustrated in relationships with other Christians.

The Dragon of Conformism teaches us to believe that "I am who others recognize me to be." When I am recognized by others, I feel great. When I am not recognized by others, I feel small. I must conform to their expectations of what is valuable or I won't feel valuable.

The Dragon of Conformism distorts our relationships. Once our sense of identity is weakened by Individualism, we look to others, becoming dependent on them, for our sense of worth.

I think of the fateful conference of national religious leaders that I mentioned in the last chapter. As I listened to the speakers I was restless, shifting in my chair, crossing and uncrossing my legs. I would put my pen down, pick it up and put it down again. I was tempted to flip the pages of my Bible and just look around the room.

I was restless, not because the speakers were poor, but because they were excellent. I should have been appreciative. Instead I was frustrated. I had spoken on the very material they were presenting. I had even written on the subject. All I could think was, "Why is he up there on the platform, and why am I down here in the audience?"

As I struggled with my feelings, I became painfully aware of how badly I wanted to be recognized. It was not a mild desire. It was a driving need. Between sessions, I was tempted to engage in a personal public relations campaign. "Hey, I know this stuff. You should be listening to me."

Wanting recognition is not necessarily wrong. We all have a need to be noticed. But the Dragon of Conformism transforms that legitimate desire into a consuming need. Jean-Paul Sartre once observed that Americans don't feel like they have arrived at personhood unless they have been given approval through public recognition.

Isolation and insecurity accompany conformism. Isolation results because, while we are always involved with others, relationships are superficial. We don't enjoy others for who they are but for the notice they give us. Insecurity arises because we must always take a poll to see how others are rating us today. Consequently, our sense of self-worth goes up and down like the stock market. Ironically, with all the emphasis on self we are seeing the decline of the "independent citizen."[1]

Acceptance

Conformism creates an insatiable need for acceptance. During college I drove a school bus. On the high-school route the "in" kids sat in the back of the bus, naturally. One student, John, was definitely not one of the insiders, but he wanted to be. Even though he was not welcome at the back, he went straight for it as soon as I picked him up. And every time he got on I wondered what would happen. He was derided, scorned, laughed at, even pushed down a time or two. But no matter what happened, John wanted to be accepted by the people in the back.

John stands out because he reminds me of myself in high school. I didn't try to push my way into the back of the bus, but as a high-school student, I was very aware that there were "in" crowds and "out" crowds. Playing guitar and growing my hair were the means I used to get "in."

After my conversion I wrote a song which expressed the frustration I felt from living under peer pressure:

Give me freedom from the crowd,
Freedom from the pressure to conform.
Give me freedom from the crowd,
Freedom from the pressure to perform.
Hey there, you in high school, are you being cool?
Did you make the football team this year?
Well, you got to wear your hair long or you got to wear it short,
Got to do what everybody tells you to.

It was my protest song, sung in the coffee houses of St. Louis in the early seventies. I sang it with a great deal of self-righteous gusto, sure that I had escaped such things and was now free of the pressure and desire to conform.

It is natural to want to be a part of a group—the garden club, bridge club, country club, fraternity or sorority. We all feel a need for affiliation. However, if acceptance in a certain group is needed to have a sense of personal worth, then we are in the clutches of the Dragon of Conformism.

Conforming

Conformism creates a need to conform. Every few years a new youth culture rises up to assert its "individuality"—long hair, bald heads, partially shaved heads, teased hair . . . but conformism is still the guiding value. To be acceptable, one still has to conform to the new group norm.

As strange as some of the styles of the youth culture may seem, they reflect the impact of conformism on our society as a whole. As I write, the hippie culture of the sixties has become the yuppie culture of the eighties. Miniskirts have given way to business suits and '55 Chevys to BMWs. While the two decades may seem different, they are much more alike than it appears. The common theme is conformism.

As our natural need to belong is distorted by the Dragon of Conformism, we become chameleons. How we see ourselves and how others see us varies depending on the group of people we happen to be with. So we change as we move from group to group.

On one level, it is natural to adopt values and tastes from those around us. That's the nature of culture. But we also have an inner standard, a personal gyroscope, that guides our decisions and actions. However, the Dragon of Conformism takes away that gyroscope and substitutes a radar system. I guide my life by sensing the expectations of others and conforming to them.

On a superficial level it may mean conforming to certain fashions, changing styles so we are acceptable to varied social circles. On a deeper level it may mean shifting moral standards. That is, when I am with Christian friends I act one way. When I am with non-Christians I may act another. The real question in both cases is, "What will people think of me?"

When I first began to face this Dragon, I discovered that I have a temptation to adjust the truth depending on the people I am speaking to. No outright lie, you understand. But a little shift here, a leaving out of some fact there, so my words would have their maximum effect. I've been more concerned about what I think others want to hear than about speaking the truth.

One of the constantly recurring questions I must deal with every year is whether it is good for Christian students to join a fraternity or sorority. The questions I ask students who want advice are, "Can you choose to do what is right, even if there is significant pressure to act in a way that is contrary to your convictions? Do you feel like you need to belong in order to feel good about yourself?"

But of course, conforming is not just a problem in fraternities or sororities. Here in the South I discover that students may join a campus Christian fellowship because lots of others do it too. In one sense, I'm glad to have people involved for any reason. However, the goal is to move students from being religious for the sake of conformity to acting from a sense of inner conviction—from a radar system to a gyroscope. If they don't, once they leave college and their Christian friends, they will simply revert to the world's way of life.

Acting as a Way of Life
Remember the scene from the movie *The Wizard of Oz* as Dorothy and her three companions tremble before the huge image of the wizard in his throne room? Clouds of smoke billow,

lightning flashes and a deep rumbling voice booms, "What do you want of the Great Oz?" Shaking in fear, they all lay their request for help before the awesome image.

That is, they trembled until Toto, Dorothy's dog, pulls back a curtain exposing a funny little man working a control panel. The Great Oz wasn't so overwhelming at all. He just learned how to cast a big image.

Like the Great Oz, we feel a need to project an image when we are possessed by conformism. As conformism creates a need in us to perform for approval, we become actors.

If I Am So Successful, Why Do I Feel Like a Fake? discusses the Imposter Phenomenon. According to the book, seventy per cent of successful individuals privately live in fear the mask of success they have constructed will be discovered. "Other people may make the 'mistake' of thinking this person is bright, creative and gifted. He remains secretly convinced that he is mediocre, un-qualified, incompetent. . . . And for some people who suffer from this syndrome, the more successful they get, the more severe and crippling it becomes."[2] Although we choose to sub-mit to the Dragon of Conformism, it is an uncomfortable way to live. We can't let others get too close. Likewise we can't let others know when we are hurting. The real "me" might be seen.

Conformism in the Church
The Dragon of Conformism has worked its way easily from the world into the church. Not only does it make it hard to have deep relationships, it weakens our ability to stand against the pressures of the world. We bend and shape our convictions and conduct so we can fit in. We are more concerned with maintain-ing a Christian image than sharing ourselves or knowing others deeply.

"How does one become great in the kingdom of God?" the

disciples asked Jesus. According to the Dragon of Conformism, the answer should be, "Recognition." The more recognition you get, the greater you are.

The church has not built many moats or raised many drawbridges against the Dragon of Conformism. In many cases we have made him an honored guest. Just like the world we find acceptance by others, performing for others and conforming to others the means and measure of our worth.

After a fragmented home life and frustrated wandering through the sixties youth culture, I grew to spiritual and emotional health in the loving attention of a small, vibrant Baptist church. There I learned that my baptism as an infant in the Episcopal church was not valid. So I was properly dunked. However, when I went to the Presbyterian seminary, I learned that I should not have been dunked; theologically, my infant baptism was acceptable to God. At the seminary I was taught to believe that most of the church's problems for the past two thousand years were because people didn't have their doctrine straight. Friends in a local charismatic community, however, assured me that in fact it was the emphasis on doctrine which was responsible for the church's present problems.

What we believe is frequently the result not of logic but of association. Each group of Christians has its own distinctives, and we are expected to conform to the group beliefs. The song, "I Want to Be a Clone" by Steve Taylor, captures the dynamic: "If you want to be one of his, got to act like one of us."

Learning our faith from others is proper. But the goal is still a spiritual gyroscope not a religious radar system. If I am expected to uncritically accept beliefs without examination and exploration, then my spiritual experience fits only an outward mold and doesn't affect my inner life.

Likewise, if conformity is our way of life in the church, it will be a way of life outside the church. There will be no inner resources to face the pressures of the world. We will lose our savor as salt and will put our lights under baskets. No, our concern must be for conviction rather then conformity.

Christian Performing

When I was given a copy of *The Holy Fool* at my recent ordination, I winced. It is a novel about a pastor who had found himself performing the role of a sanctified Christian leader while having lost the reality of his faith. Was my friend giving me a subtle hint or blatant warning? Because of the Dragon of Conformism we can become performers in a holy play before the church and world.

I confess that I do catch myself seeking to project an image of a "Christian leader." My small group and prayer partner help me be honest. When I am busy displaying my theological knowledge and ministerial competence, they occasionally say to me, "Come on, how is it really going?" Without them I would be condemned to spiritual superficiality; keeping up an image would put a wall between me and the fellowship that I need.

One lie the Dragon of Conformism whispers in our ears is that we must project an image of a "good" Christian so we will have a good witness. "You have to be attractive if you are to attract people to Christ." Or we might hear it in the form of, "Come join our church. It is the largest in the area, with the largest choir. There is special music in every service and major speakers from around the country every Sunday evening." Unfortunately, such witness wilts as it is exposed to real life. Exhaustion and isolation set in from projecting an image that displays only the smiles and "blessings." Churches too easily have revolving doors with disillusioned people walking out because they heard about all the great things that would happen if they followed Christ. But no one prepared them for the struggles that come with spiritual growth.

Because of the Dragon of Conformism we confuse spiritual authority with popularity. Widespread acceptance means widespread credibility. The larger a leader's following, the greater authority we give him. If he has lots of followers, he must be right. The danger is that there is little evaluation of the quality and content of the message.

In the same confusion, but with a slightly different twist, we make converted celebrities into religious authorities. It doesn't matter how long they have been Christians. Because of their celebrity status, we accord them a receptive audience.

Taming the Dragon of Conformism

To escape from the Dragon of Conformism we need to conform more closely to God's view of who we are and how valuable we are. As we grow in dependence on him, we can discover a freedom to be ourselves that leads to healthy relationships.

Saul was in big trouble. God promised him victory over the Amalekites but warned him not to take any of the spoils. After the victory Saul bent the rule a little and allowed his army to keep a few things—sheep, cattle, a few gold trinkets. When Samuel showed up after the battle he pronounced judgment. Saul would lose his throne. Saul's response to Samuel displays the source of his problem: "I was afraid of the people and so I gave in to them" (1 Sam 15:24).

Even after the severe judgment, Saul still doesn't seem to grasp the source of his problem. He begs Samuel to keep up appearances. "I have sinned. But please honor me before the elders of my people and before Israel; come back with me, that I may worship the LORD your God" (1 Sam 15:30). Caving into peer pressure was a pattern in Saul's life. It made him a poor king and cost his family the royal line.

In Saul we see the destructive results of being socially dependent. Yet in Saul we are pointed in the direction of the remedy—a respect for (the Old Testament calls it a fear of) the Lord that places God above everyone else, no matter what the cost, no matter what others may think. The issue is not what do others think of me, but what does God think of me.

Jesus calls us to turn away from dependence on others to a radical dependence on God. He warned against the dangers of conformity. "Do not be afraid of those who kill the body but cannot kill the soul. Rather, be afraid of the one who can destroy both soul and body in hell" (Mt 10:28). A stern word from a loving person. Whether conformity for fear of death or just rejection, the root issue is the same—someone else is setting my agenda. Jesus knew that we cannot give priority to God if we give priority to others.

Likewise, Jesus warned about the dangers of performing. "Be careful not to do your 'acts of righteousness' before men, to be seen by them" (Mt 6:1). He goes on to warn about praying before others, giving alms before others and fasting before others. Those who do these before others get their reward—recognition. But there is a greater reward, a heavenly one for those whose motivation is vertical rather then horizontal.

Ananias and Sapphira are an object lesson against performing for the sake of the saints. Conformism leads them to lie. They sold land and gave it to the church. That was a good thing to do; lots of others were doing it too. Only Ananias and Sapphira wanted to look really good. They lied about the price and the little profit they were making on the side. The judgment administered through Peter seems harsh, but it is in the Scriptures. They died.

Performing was a problem in the New Testament church and

has been one we have struggled with throughout our history. Saint Syncletice, an abbess whose wisdom was recorded in "The Sayings of the Fathers" taught, "An open treasury is quickly spent. And any virtue will be annihilated if it is published abroad and becomes famous." She also taught, "The same thing cannot at once be seed and full grown bush. So men with a worldly reputation cannot bear heaven's fruit."[3]

As God's people, we are to live in complete dependence on God. Yet this dependence on God does not exclude others. Rather it frees us for relationships. I am not suggesting that we go back to an unhealthy individualism. There is a dynamic balance and a need for discernment. This is part of the mystery of knowing God among his people. Totally dependent on him, we are free to know him in relation to others.

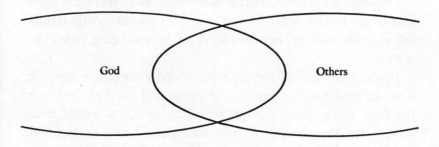

Figure 7. The Balance of God and Others

In our culture this is difficult. We don't seem to be able to live in the balance. Our natural tendency is to be pulled out of the center in the direction of others.

The Discipline of Solitude
Solitude is the spiritual discipline that strikes at our distorted dependence on others. Through solitude we separate ourselves

from others to be with God. And through solitude we can grow into healthy relationships with others. For those afflicted with conformism, solitude is not natural. It is threatening to be alone when we are so totally dependent on others.

Throughout the history of the church, those who sought after godliness have found solitude a helpful spiritual discipline. The desert fathers were pioneers in the use of solitude. But the use of the desert did not originate with them. The desert is a recurring motif in the Scriptures. Isaac, Moses, David, Elijah, John the Baptist, Jesus and Paul all left their familiar world to meet God alone in the desert.

The experience of solitude is rich and varied. I want to mention two ways to begin developing this discipline—corporate solitude and personal solitude.

Corporate Solitude. Abraham was called away from his home and family to follow God to an unknown country. Although he left with his wife, nephew and servants, he was being called into solitude.

Israel, after leaving Egypt, experienced a corporate solitude. They left the familiar patterns of Egypt and lived in the desert for forty years. (Even though returning to Egypt would mean slavery, the Dragon called them back many times during their journey to the Promised Land.)

The disciples of Jesus were called to leave their family and vocation. Although they were surrounded by others, they too were called into solitude.

These are all experiences of solitude because solitude is not first of all separation from others, but a moving away from those we have depended on so we can move into a deeper dependence on God. They all left their familiar world and supports behind. They cast themselves on God.

If we are sensitive, we will discover that God brings such

experiences of solitude into our lives periodically. It may come as a move from one place to another such as going off to college or taking a job in a new city. These times of adjustment often bring a sense of loneliness that God uses to draw us into deeper dependence on him.

Or it may be that we move into a period of dry relationships. For some reason that we can't quite figure out, we feel separated from our family and friends. Try what we will, we can't seem to escape a sense of isolation. Going to church, meeting friends, visiting relatives, all seem to have a dry sawdust quality about them.

Much of seminary was a desert experience for me. My initial response was to blame my professors and the school. I was sure they weren't doing something right. It seemed that God was distant, and I couldn't seem to develop satisfying relationships even though I had several good friends.

These desert times are uncomfortable, and we usually try to escape them as soon as possible. Instead we should receive the sense of separation as a gift from God. When we settle into it, we can allow God to do a deep work of inner freedom in our hearts. Toward the end of seminary, I discovered a new faith in God, an internal faith that was mine, not something I was imitating.

Personal Solitude. Being separated from others when they are nearby is a painful type of solitude for me. I find personal solitude much more enjoyable. Richard Rolle, an English mystic of the fourteenth century, described his experience of God as "clearest sweetness."[4]

In conferences I direct, I often schedule a retreat of solitude. Everyone is sent off alone for three hours just to be with God. Initially this seems intimidating. "What am I going to do for three hours of sitting by myself?" However, as we discuss it afterward, people share about a rich time with God. Some speak of a sense of refreshing hunger for God welling up inside. Others speak of an enticing presence. On the other hand, some share frustrations and a sense of emptiness. I know these times too. In these cases I hasten to give encouragement. Even in the echoing silence, there is spiritual profit in a heart reaching after God.

Solitude is not limited to extended times of spiritual reflection. It can be as short as a ten-minute break in your schedule. Just relax into the presence of God with a seeking heart.

Since solitude is God's gift, it often comes unexpectedly. Initially you may be taking a break, just to clear your head and discover a refreshing sense of Someone with you.

Contentment
Discontent is the mark of the Dragons of Individualism and Conformism. Discontent marks the search for self that is so much a part of our world. In contrast, the experience of a radical dependence on God and the spiritual bond with God's people leads to contentment.

First, we can be content with ourselves. Have you ever tried to keep a child's toy ball inflated when it has a tiny leak? Slowly but certainly it deflates, and you have to constantly blow into it to keep it inflated. The self-image created by the Dragons is an inflated one, and one with a leak in it. We must try by every way we can to keep it filled up, but of course it is consuming and hopeless. We fear that if all the air comes out there won't be anything left of us. That is, of course, not true. We will just shrink down to our proper size, the size God has made us to be. What a relief when we don't have to be working to keep our image inflated. There is new energy to enjoy life. We can enjoy others, enjoy God and enjoy ourselves.

Second, when we have tamed the Dragons we can be content

How We See Conformism

Conformism wants me to believe:	"I am who others recognize me to be."
How conformism is seen in the world:	Perpetual public relations
How conformism is seen in the church:	Spiritual public relations

How We Defeat Conformism

The biblical value to combat conformism:	Individuality—"God knows me."
The spiritual discipline to combat conformism:	Solitude
The result of defeating conformism:	Contentment

Figure 8. Defeating Conformism

with others. We can enjoy being a part of his people without being in a dependant bondage to them. I may still have desires that are not being met, but it's okay. God's Spirit can give me what I need. Instead of seeking to extract recognition or approval, I can know that God will meet me as I extend myself to his people. Inside we all have needs and I can be content sharing needs, not eradicating them.

Finally, when we have tamed the Dragons, we can be content with God. Sitting at home in the quiet after children are in bed, during a lunch break in a deserted office, even driving home from a busy day, there is a "full silence" available to us. The root meaning of the word *contentment* is to be self-contained. As we turn to God we can have an internal sense of self that is true contentment.

For Individuals and Groups

1. How does conformism make our sense of worth dependent on the

opinions of others?

2. Give an example of how the Dragon of Conformism creates a need for acceptance from others, conforming to the expectations of others or acting as a way of life.

3. What is the difference between having a personal radar system or an inner gyroscope (pp. 82-83)?

4. Mention some of the ways that the Dragon of Conformism has invaded the church.

5. How can seeking to project a good image (personally or corporately) in order to be a witness create a serious problem?

6. What other ways can the Dragon of Conformism hinder our ability to witness with integrity?

7. How can the Dragon of Conformism create a false aura of religious authority?

8. What is wrong with having a religious radar system?

9. How does the character of Saul display the problems of conformism as a way of life (pp. 87-88)?

10. In what ways does dependence on God strike at the heart of conformism?

11. How is the discipline of solitude a way to help us confront our tendency toward conformism?

12. Describe your understanding of corporate and personal solitude.

13. When you experienced corporate solitude, what was it like? How did you deal with it?

14. What are some ways that you can begin to practice the discipline of solitude?

15. The Dragons of Individualism and Conformism ravage our lives with discontent. Describe the sense of contentment that can fill our lives when we have faced them.

6
The Dragon of Relativism

Facing Life with a Confident Faith

Helen leans against Russ and cries, her face full of pain. I swallow hard and look down at the floor. All around the room people are crying. My thoughts are rambling and disjointed, "What am I doing here? Why did this have to happen?"

This is a memorial service for Anthony. He is the second infant to die in four months in our little church. I can't know the depth of the pain of grieving parents, but I hurt too. I remind myself, somehow, that in some way God is in control. The deaths don't make much sense to us, but even so they are not outside the purpose of God.

In the service there is a time for sharing. Members of our congregation speak to Russ and Helen, offering words of compassion and concern. As we comfort them, they comfort us. Russ and Helen assure us that one day they will see Anthony in eternity and know the joy they missed in this life being his parents.

Spoken through tears, these words are more than pious phrases. They are spoken in the midst of pain, spoken from the heart and spoken in faith.

We need faith. From it we derive the courage to face life, to reach out to others, to see the good in our trials and to not be overwhelmed by them. But for faith to be strong enough to sustain us, it must be built on a strong foundation. Only God is sufficient. Everything else is too small, too limited, too weak.

There is, however, a Dragon, a good, solid, patriotic value that removes faith from its foundation, the Dragon of Relativism. He makes faith sufficient all by itself. He says that faith has a power all its own. It is not important what you believe in, only that you believe.

On a personal level his message to us is, "I am whatever I want to believe." He offers a pragmatic, worldly faith that provides power to reshape ourselves and our environment to fit our desires. It is not necessary, he says, to believe in some spiritual being we can't see or moral standards that make us uncomfortable. If we focus our faith on what we can see and what we want, then we can tap into the unknown powers within us. But the faith of the Dragon of Relativism is a faith that is built on air. He offers us strength to face life without anything solid to back it up.

The Dragon of Relativism leaves a vacuum which opens the door for the other Dragons. Because we have no foundation for our faith, we often believe what others believe (conformism). We believe what we want to believe (individualism). We believe whatever will get us the most money (materialism). And because deep down we aren't really sure of anything, we work hard at everything (activism).

The church has rightly sought to expose this Dragon's deception. But we haven't escaped his enchantment. Too often we have been tricked into looking to faith for strength rather than to God. Even if we do manage to focus on God, our faith is often shaky. We become negative and defensive, and the church fragments with suspicion everywhere.

The Power of Positive Faith

Relative faith is an integral part of the success ethic. Along with work it is the means to prosperity. The author of *Think and Grow Rich* writes, "Directed faith makes every thought crackle with power. You can rise to limitless heights, impelled by the lifting of your mighty new self-confidence."[1] The Dragon of Relativism tells us that whatever we choose to believe will come true for us. As another put it, "To think success brings success."[2]

Relative faith is an important part of North American thinking. The book *The Power of Positive Thinking* published in the fifties is a part of a long tradition. It inspires us to do our best and tap the depths of our energy and ability. In the 1920s the teaching of a Frenchman swept through North America. He advocated repeating the phrase "Day by day, in every way, I am getting better and better."[3]

I am attracted to such an approach to life. One of my favorite stories as a boy was "The Little Train That Could." It is about a little train that needs to take a large load to some children over the mountain because the big train, which was supposed to do it, is broken. Although it is too small it takes on the task and repeats as it goes up the incline, "I think I can. I think I can. I think I can." I would strain with the little train as it chugged up the mountain and always had a sense of victory when it made it. I would love to repeat with the train as it went down the other side, "I thought I could. I thought I could. I thought I could . . ."

I enjoyed the story and read it over and over. The moral of

taking on big tasks with a positive attitude has inspired me at points in my life. Looking for the bright side of things, I've been helped to keep going when times were tough.

But in the end I found that the faith it inspired was a problem. Although I don't like to admit it, there are mountains which were too high for me. When I tried to climb some of them, I came crashing down. I learned painfully that my faith and determination alone were insufficient. Faith in success left me in despair over my weakness.

Even though the Dragon of Relativism makes faith in faith inadequate to meet life's challenges, it is the only thing the world has to offer. Don Quixote and Willy Loman are symbols of our time. The theme of *The Man from LaMancha* was, "To dream the impossible dream, to reach the unreachable star." Don Quixote was a man of faith, perhaps a suitable romantic hero for a relativistic culture. But he spent his life jousting windmills and pledging himself to a prostitute.

Willy Loman, the tragic character of *The Death of a Salesman,* had faith too. Somehow he was sure that if he just kept believing and selling he could be successful. His faith, however, kept him from confronting his own weakness and failures. When reality finally did break through, he was driven to suicide. "I am what I believe," did not work for Willy Loman.

What if we are exceptionally gifted, and through determination and strong faith become high achievers? Without sufficient grounding eventually we will live beyond our means. Outwardly we may achieve success, but inside there is a creeping hollowness created by the use of resources that we could not afford to spend. We become like a house of cards with our accomplishments precariously balanced against each other and in impending danger of collapse. The unhealthy intensity of our faith burns us out. In the end faith is abused and lost.

The faith of the Dragon of Relativism is too limited. It is a worldly faith that provides no strength to face the ups and downs of life, including death. Russ and Helen do not draw their strength from faith in faith, but from faith in God.

Relative Truth

How did the Dragon of Relativism grow to have such influence and power? He rises from the cultivated soil of a relative view of truth.

Standing on the edge of a large crowd of several hundred people I hear a student say, "What is true for you may not be true for me. Why ask me to believe in your understanding of God?" In the center of the crowd is Cliffe Knechtle, a skillful discussion leader on issues related to Christianity. I have asked him to come to campus to make Christianity a campuswide issue. It seems to be working. Students on the edges listen skeptically, but many in the center have been listening and talking for an hour or more.

This is the third day of these noon-hour discussions. As I have listened to the questions and spoken with students, it seems that I have heard that objection repeatedly that truth is personal and each person must find out what is true for himself or herself.

As a culture we have given up believing that there is certain unchanging truth about ultimate issues. God, life after death, meaning and purpose, right and wrong—there are no answers to these issues that can be known.

The university, the institution in our world which has historically been devoted to the search for truth is the place where a belief in truth is frequently lost. Many students come to campus with a vague belief system. In the university they examine the foundations of faith in a search for truth. This is proper. We do need to think about the place of truth and the reasons why we believe. However, what frequently comes through is that, since truth can't be scientifically examined, it can't be known. This materialistic view of truth requires that something be measurable before it can be known. The whole spiritual side of reality is lost and with it access to truth.

When a belief in truth is taken away, generally nothing is put in its place. Our inborn urge to have faith finds no object. So it turns back on itself. A four-lane highway is paved into our hearts for the Dragon of Relativism to drive on.

Relative Morals

Relative truth leads to relative morals. "Since I am what I believe," the Dragon of Relativism convinces us, "I may do whatever I believe."

As I listened to the discussions with Cliffe on campus, another issue surfaced repeatedly. I hear people say, "It is not right to set moral standards by which everyone is judged. Moral behavior is a personal issue. You can't say that the way you act is right and the way I act is wrong."

Robert Ringer's *Looking Out for Number One* captures the mood of the world so well. The flames of the Dragon of Relativism leap from his pages. "Clear your mind, then. Forget the foundationless traditions, forget the 'moral' standards others may have tried to cram down your throat, forget the beliefs people may have tried to intimidate you into accepting as 'right.' "[4]

It is this type of relative thinking that has sent tremors and quakes through our culture. It is supposed to be liberating, but it is destructive. Every culture has had to deal with lawbreakers. But the Dragon of Relativism has changed that. The moral foundations of law are gone. People may still break laws, but no longer need to consider themselves truly guilty. The only crime they need to worry about is getting caught.

Watergate is the symbol of a culture being scorched by the Dragon—lawbreaking in the name of a personal cause. If we believe that there is no moral standard of right and wrong, then we are free to do as we please, even if we have to break a few laws. In government, business, personal issues, in any area, we are free to "forget the moral standards others have tried to cram down our throats."

Even if there are no scandals and we commit no crimes, we suffer from relative morality. While we do what we want, we are never sure of ourselves. There is no certain standard by which we can chart our actions. We are like navigators with no stars by which we may mark our direction. We live with a gnawing doubt that we have missed something, that we have made a wrong turn.

This internal conflict, this vague sense of guilt arises because there is an inner sense of what is right and what is wrong that we cannot escape. We may do what we want, but deep down we probably don't feel good about it.

The beguiling dominance of this Dragon is everywhere. Even those who don't buy his line feel his pressure. I wince frequently when I watch movies or television—not just because I see immoral behavior but because those who dare object are portrayed as old-fashioned, judgmental, inhibited and hypocritical. The plot always compels me to sympathize with the hero who seeks to throw off the outmoded morality of some shriveled sourpuss who wants to spoil everyone's fun. And all this despite my convictions! Who wants to be on the side of a hypocrite?

The Dragon of Relativism affects our relationships with others as well. Because beliefs and behavior are so personalized, there is little common ground with others. There is little basis for in-depth communication. The "I-know-what-you-mean" experience becomes rare. My moral system, my faith is just mine. Your faith, your moral system is yours. Where there is overlap, we connect. But the more relativized we are, the less overlap there is.

We speak to each from islands floating in a sea covered with fog. Occasionally we bump into others who may be in the same current we are in, but eventually the islands separate and we are on our own again. Life becomes a series of bumps for limited periods of time.

Dragons in the Church

The faith that provides strength for life is the faith of the historic Christian church, faith in God through Jesus Christ. However, the church is not immune to the Dragon of Relativism. On the contrary, Christians are extremely susceptible. As the Dragon infiltrates the church he leaches out the content and leaves an empty shell of faith. We think we have Christian faith when we only have the faith of the Dragon of Relativism.

We see his effects in the intense faith of a "positive confession," in the vague faith of those who aren't certain what they believe, in the dogmatic faith of defensive believers, and in the timid expressions of a private faith. Let's look at each in turn.

Positive Confession. Lisa's eyebrows knit together and her lips are pursed tight in exasperation. She is telling me about an experience she had recently in the hospital. A well-meaning Christian friend offered comfort by suggesting that Lisa's illness was an indication that she lacked faith. Her friend suggested that Lisa could be cured if she just would believe.

The result of the friend's help was not comfort for Lisa but confusion. As far as Lisa knew, she was trusting God to the best of her ability. What more was she supposed to do? Lisa was a victim of someone with a Christian form of relative faith. The

Dragon of Relativism tells us that if we believe something hard enough God will make it happen. There is a subtle shift here that can slip right by us if we aren't careful. God is still in the equation but the focus of faith is still faith and not God. He becomes an instrument of our faith rather than the object of our faith. The Almighty, the foundation of our faith, quietly slipped into the background.

One expression of relativized faith is that of "positive confession." Advocates teach, "If you want it, if you believe God for it and if you say it, then you can have it." Or more crassly, "Name it and claim it."[5] Don Cosset titles his book on the subject *What You Say Is What You Get*. In the background I hear the Dragon of Relativism muttering, "I am what I believe."

My two boys, Jeremy and Chris, frequently come up with plans for me to take them out for ice cream. However, no matter how intensely they seek to convince themselves, and me, that this is what I am going to do, there are times when I say no. My decision is not based only on the intensity of their faith that I will do it (although I confess it does influence me), but also on what is best for them. Surely our heavenly father works the same way!

Disillusion and despair are close behind this work of the Dragon. Rather than giving strength to live, he sets us up for a fall. When the postive confession doesn't get us what we want, as will surely happen, we must conclude that there is something wrong with God or us. Either we aren't believing hard enough or God has left us. For sincere people, either choice is depressing.

Vague Faith. In a committee meeting with representatives from several different churches, a disquiet is building up inside me. I hold back as long as I can, but I'm going to have to say something soon, and when I do, I know its going to be a bomb.

The purpose of the committee is to discuss a cooperative approach to campus ministry. As we discuss objectives for the committee phrases like "spiritual needs" and "ministry to the whole person" are tossed around the room. I'm not sure how these phrases are being used so I offer more specific terms, "faith in Jesus Christ" and "the lordship of Jesus Christ over every area of life."

. . . Just as I feared. There is a stunned silence in the room.

I transgressed the unwritten rule. Since we were from several different churches with different approaches to Christianity, we are supposed to be as broad as possible. And somehow shifting the discussion from spiritual needs to faith in Christ was too specific.

After the initial shock the discussion got hot. The meeting ended before we reached a consensus. I am not sure where we will go from here. We have more talking to do before we get past our reactions and down to our real concerns.

Unjustified or not, my concerns were triggered by my battle with the Dragon of Relativism. He would have us believe that faith in God need not be specific. Any kind of faith is sufficient. Again, notice the subtle shift. In contrast to the faith of a positive confession, God is still the object of faith, but the content of the word *God* vanishes. God can be whoever, or whatever, we conceive him to be.

Since we can't know anything for certain about God, the Dragon of Relativism would have us believe that any kind of sincere faith will do. But I know it will not. I spoke out because the meeting sounded too much like the church experience of my childhood. Although my parents took me to church as a child and I was active through my early teen years, I never heard about the necessity of faith in Christ as a means to spiritual life. Somehow all I got from my church attendance was the Dragon's

message, "Whatever I believe about God is sufficient, just as long as I am sincere."

But when my mother developed cancer and the family began to come apart, I was not prepared. I found no strength in a vague contentless faith. I left the church to look for answers somewhere else. It was not till several years later and several blind alleys that I found the content of faith in Christ that provided the answers and resources I needed.

Dogmatic Faith. Even though our faith may be in God who is more than a good feeling, who is the Creator of Time and Space and the Sovereign of the Universe, we can still be affected by the Dragon of Relativism. Our sense of confidence can still be shaken. We must deal with doubts, often very subtle, which gnaw at us. The result can be a defensive dogmatism.

The Christian college I attended was founded in 1966. It was a break off from a college that had been founded in 1956 that was part of a denomination that had been founded a few years before from a denomination formed in the 1930s. Each group was certain that it was right before the Lord and that the other was clearly in the wrong.

Sermon notes of St. Jerome in the fourth century had a note scribbled in the margin, "Weak point. Shout louder." Instead of a confident view of life based on what we know of God, we become defensively aggressive. Our whole approach to life becomes not who we can put our faith in but what we are (or who we are) against.

Sitting in the student union, Laura told me that she was pulling out of the Christian fellowship. She had recently come to conclusions about baptism that she felt were absolutely essential. Since not everyone in the fellowship shared her view, she felt that she could no longer participate. It didn't matter that she shared a common Savior, a common love of the Scriptures, a common concern for sharing her faith. She was separating herself because she thought she had truth and the others didn't. I was sorry to see her leave. She is a friend I will miss. Her insecurities, foisted on her by the Dragon of Relativism, has made her defensively dogmatic. I shake my head as I think, "Another one scorched by the Dragon."

Timid Faith. The Dragon of Relativism can also make us uncomfortable about sharing our faith with others. The flip side of dogmatic faith is private faith. We don't tell others what to believe. We don't even tell others what we believe!

Since the general attitude of the world inspired by the Dragon of Relativism is that people have their own truth, we fear we will be perceived as out of order if we speak of certain truth in a God who is there. A book by Don Posterski on evangelism is called *Why Am I Afraid to Tell You I'm a Christian?* Good title. It describes exactly how we can feel about our faith because of the work of the Dragon of Relativism. Although we may affirm that we have a faith that is true for all, we end up acting as if it is only true for me.

Taming the Dragon of Relativism

We need faith. We can't live without it. But the faith the Dragon of Relativism produces is insufficient. We need faith, a faith in God which is sure and certain.

Despite the Dragon of Relativism, we need not be trapped in positive confession, vague faith, dogmatic faith or timid faith. We can have faith in God because he has spoken to us in the Scriptures. If we are to draw strength from faith we must recover what the Dragon of Relativism has destroyed—faith that is confidently yet humbly based in the Bible.

For the Christian, God and the Bible go hand in hand. It is impossible to separate them. Without the Scriptures we are at the mercy of the Dragon of Relativism, we are without a sufficient focus for our faith. We can be strong in our belief in God precisely because we have a strong foundation in the Bible.

What does it mean that the Bible is the Word of God? This is an essential question for a church attacked by the Dragon of Relativism. A vague concept of the Bible leads to vague faith. Because God and the Scriptures are so intimately tied together, we need to consider how we approach them. How can a book written over a period of more than a thousand years by dozens of men be God's Word? How can it be significant in my life today? And if it is God's Word, how come there are so many disagreements among Christians?

Word and Spirit

God has spoken by words that have been written down. The apostle Paul writes, "All Scripture is God-breathed and is useful . . ." (2 Tim 3:16). This is God's pattern of revelation from the beginning, speaking to his people through prophets, teachers and apostles. This is what God's people have believed for over three thousand years. Because we have his words in writing, we have something clear and certain to read and through which we can grow in faith.

But God's Word is not limited to words written down in the past. God opens our spiritual eyes and ears so that we may meet him on the pages of Scripture. The apostle Paul writes to those in Ephesus, "I keep asking that the God of our Lord Jesus Christ, the glorious Father, may give you the Spirit of wisdom and revelation, so that you may know him better. I pray also that the eyes of your heart may be enlightened in order that you may know the hope to which he has called you" (Eph 1:17-18). Paul knew that his own teaching was not enough. God must make it plain. And so it is with all the Scriptures.

We must keep these two sides of God's revelation in balance. The historic formula of the church is Word *and* Spirit. We can know the Scriptures from front to back and still not know God. The Pharisees and Sadducees knew books of Scripture by heart, but they still were spiritually blind.

On the other hand, if we look only to the Spirit apart from the written Word, we are in spiritual danger. The history of the church is littered with those whose faith has been shipwrecked by personal revelations that go beyond the Scriptures. The written Word is our sure foundation.

Past yet Present

The God of the Scriptures is a God of history. If we are to understand the Bible correctly, we must see it as a book dealing with history. We read the Bible to understand what has happened between God and his people in the past. As we read it, however, we discover that the Scriptures are also a book of the present.

At the end of forty years of wilderness wandering, Moses stood before the people of Israel. As he prepares them to enter the Promised Land, he mentions the way God led them at the start of their forty-year journey. "Then the LORD spoke to you out of the fire. You heard the sound of words . . ." (Deut 4:12). What is significant about this scene is that Moses is speaking to a new generation of Israel, one that was not present at Mt. Sinai when God spoke from the fire and gave them the Law. But the Words of God have an eternal quality about them. Spoken to one generation, they have significance for every generation.

Likewise we find that he speaks to us through what he said to his people in the past. Their experience with God becomes a means for me to understand my experience with God. Abraham in a foreign land, Joseph in prison, Joshua leading Israel into the

Promised Land, David being chosen by God, David in the desert fleeing Saul, Jesus in Gethsemane . . . the Scriptures provide us with pattern after pattern of people who have trusted God.

Revelation and Response

If we are to benefit from the Scriptures, we must also see that our understanding is affected by our own experience. How we understand the Bible will be colored by the age and culture we live in, by our family background and our own personality.

There are significant differences in the church. There is Reformed theology and Arminian theology, Lutheran theology and Catholic theology. There is the Methodist Church, the Episcopal Church, the Presbyterian Church, the Pentecostal Church and . . . There are differences concerning the role of the Holy Spirit, the mode and time of baptism, when and how Christ will return, a Christian's role in politics, whether Christians can justify war . . . The list could go on and on. Who's right? Who really has the truth?

One way to handle the differences is to conclude that only you and your group are enlightened by God and that everyone else is not. I think that is a serious mistake.

Another way is to see that we each bring our own set of "filters" to the Scriptures. These filters help some to see things more clearly than others. Someone with the gift of compassion will see the emphasis on service in the Scriptures. Someone with a heart for evangelism will see the themes of witness. Someone with a lot of money may see the themes of stewardship while some in need may see the themes of caring for the poor. Someone who is spontaneous will see the importance of depending on the Spirit while someone who is very orderly will see the need for careful planning. Brought together we all see truth from the Scriptures that we can't see by ourselves. Brought together, we can grow beyond ourselves into whom God intends us to be.

But what happens when we build a whole system of truth based on only our own insights into the Scriptures? Fragmentation! We need to see that we have much more in common in the Scriptures than we have differences. Despite differences on baptism, the Scriptures teach that it is necessary. Despite differences concerning war, the Scriptures teach that murder is wrong. Despite differences on the work of the Holy Spirit, we see from the Scriptures that he is present with us and is the agent for God's work in our lives.

I am not suggesting that each position held by differing parties on divisive issues is right. That's relativism. Nor am I suggesting sloppy thinking that says it doesn't matter what you believe as long as you are sincere. That's relativism too. Nor am I suggesting that we shouldn't take a position at all. And I am certainly not suggesting that there are no essential beliefs upon which God has established the Christian faith.

I am suggesting that we hold some of our cherished positions in humility knowing that there are godly people out there who have studied the same Scriptures and come to different conclusions. We must wait for the full revelation of God when Christ returns to get some of these differences cleared up.

We need not be unsettled that the Scriptures are distorted as well as illumined by our reception, although we must struggle with this. We must remember that the Bible leads us back to the One who has spoken to us. Even if we don't know the answers, he does. Our faith is never ultimately in what we know, but in the One who knows us. So we need not fear theology. Let us study doctrine with our eyes on the One to whom all study leads.

If we are to find in the Scriptures the resources for life, then we must be careful how we approach them. We must approach them with a balanced perspective.

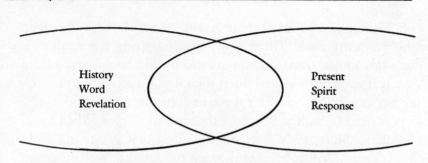

History   Present
Word   Spirit
Revelation   Response

Figure 9. The Balance of Word and Spirit

It is by faith that we keep the balance. Through faith we keep history and the present in balance, through faith we keep the Word and Spirit in balance, and by faith we keep God's revelation and our reception in balance. Extremes hurt us. Balanced faith energizes us.

The Sword That Slays the Dragon

If we are to take advantage of the Scriptures as a resource for faith in God, we must study them. It is not enough that we believe that the Bible is the Word of God. As we do so, the Scriptures become a sword that slays the Dragon of Relativism.

Since the Scriptures are the means that God has given to know him, it would seem obvious that we should study the Scriptures for ourselves. But too often we study around the Bible rather than study it. We read books about the Bible, commentaries and devotionals. We listen to teachers in the pulpit, on tapes and on the radio who tell us what the Bible says. But we don't study the Scriptures for ourselves. The result is that we lose the direct personal interaction we need with God on a regular basis. Our faith naturally tends to become vague.

When I lead seminars on how to study the Bible, no one is allowed to bring a commentary. Even study Bibles are frowned on. The tendency is to let these become the authority rather than the Scripture itself. There is joy in discovering the truth of a passage on our own. If some questions can't be answered from the text even after some effort, then it is time to consult a reference book. But only after we have done our own work.

We need to look at Scripture through fresh eyes. When I lead inductive Bible study discussions, I find that people miss obvious central truths because they are too familiar with a passage to actually see what is there. Familiarity breeds blindness. But if we are open to learn new things about God each time we come to his Word, we find new sources of faith and strength. I have been studying and teaching from the Gospel of Matthew for five years. I am always amazed at ways that I learn more about Jesus, more about the Gospel and more about myself.

We need to concentrate our study. We read a passage in a Gospel in the morning, and an epistle at night. Abba Isaac, a desert father of the fifth century, criticized monks for this same tendency. "And so it goes on, hopping from text to text, from psalm to psalm, from Gospel to Epistle and thence to a prophetic book and thence from a narrative in the historical books on the Old Testament; meandering vaguely through the Bible, choosing nothing and grasping nothing on purpose, considering no text to its depth; the mind becomes a dilettante, a taster of spiritual meanings, not a creator or owner of them."[6] We would experience the life-giving power of the Scriptures more often if we would discipline ourselves to stick with a passage until it was worked into our lives.

Instead of focusing on verses and chapters, we need to study by whole books. Not to do so is a serious mistake. How many of us would pick up a novel, read a few pages in the middle and then put the book down complaining that we couldn't understand it? Each book of the Bible, while part of the whole, is also a self-contained unit meant to be understood on its own.

When we read any book we assume that the author has a point to make. And if we miss the author's point, then we haven't understood the book. The same is true of books in the Bible. Every author in the Bible has a point to make. Recently during a seminar on the book of Matthew I told the group, "If you miss the author's point, you miss the point!" I got sighs and groans, but I was understood. Sometimes the point is implicit. Sometimes it is explicit. But it is always there. For example, even though Matthew, Mark and Luke shared much of the same material, each had a different emphasis on the ministry of Jesus.

When we study the Scriptures, we need to look for the obvious. How often we are guilty of falling into the missing-the-forest-for-the-trees syndrome. More often than not the author's point is right on the surface. We are so busy looking for a spiritual meaning that we look right past the obvious, but central, truth. Simple questions like, "What is the subject of this chapter?" or, "Who are the people involved in this passage?" do amazing things to bring the truth of the Scriptures into focus. After we have observed what is there, interpreting and applying a passage are much more fruitful.

Confidence in the Face of Life

"Because I believe that the Bible is the Word of God, I commend you to God and the Word of his grace." All around the room there were red eyes, some cried openly. Bill, our pastor, was making his final sermon. Some ten years ago as a seminary student he had begun the church. During those ten years it had grown remarkably—in quality if not in size. Compassion ministries, small groups, spiritual development, refreshing worship, world missions—how did a church of one hundred twenty have so much going on? Bill's vision and his training were at the foundation of the church. And now he was leaving. And we, Bill and his family included, were all grieving.

But we all had a sense of being on the threshold of new growth and opportunities. Bill would be joining his skills and vision with others in creative ways in Cincinnati. We in the church were sharing a deeper sense of responsibility.

Confidence to face life comes from faith in the God of the Scriptures. Bill was free to leave. We were free to let him leave because we knew that he was not the key to our growth or survival. God was, and God was not going anywhere.

As Bill spoke I was reminded of the apostle Paul in his farewell address to the Ephesian elders. "Now I commit you to God and to the word of his grace . . ." (Acts 20:32). The example of the apostle provided the pattern for us. He trusted his life-long work to God. And so must we all.

At one point in my ministry, I faced a crisis which threatened to tear an Inter-Varsity chapter wide open. The chapter had an interesting but uneasy mix of charismatic and noncharismatic students. Toward the end of the spring semester one speaker (invited by the charismatics) informed the entire chapter that all Christians had to speak in tongues. Of course his talk polarized the two groups. Several years of work looked like it was coming apart before my eyes. All I knew to do was turn to the Scriptures.

The following week I stood with this same group of students and made a fifteen-minute presentation listing all the Scriptures that dealt with the Holy Spirit and tongues. I informed them that sincere Christians took different positions on these issues. Most of us, I went on, tended to interpret Scripture the way those we respected most interpreted Scripture. I then dismissed the group to study the passages on their own for the next week. Through prayer and study the students were to formulate their own convictions about the Spirit from the Scriptures. But they

How We See Relativism

Relativism wants me to believe:	"I am whatever I want to believe."
How relativism is seen in the world:	Positive thinking, uncertain truth
How relativism is seen in the church:	Positive faith, uncertain faith

How We Defeat Relativism

The biblical value to combat relativism:	Revelation—"God shows himself to me."
The spiritual discipline to combat relativism:	Bible study
The result of defeating relativism:	Confidence

Figure 10. Defeating Relativism

were to then accord respect to those who studied the passages and came to different conclusions. I encouraged the two groups to discuss their results with each other, but admonished them to try not to proselytize those they disagreed with.

The result? The chapter became a healthy combination of different opinions with a common faith in Jesus Christ and a submission to the Bible. The two sides worked together in a creative force that presented a powerful witness to Christ.

We do not have to have all the answers when we are trusting the One who does. We do not have to have enough strength to face a tragedy when we know the One who will strengthen us. We do not have to be afraid of taking risks and trying new things when we know the Redeemer who specializes in saving people. We do not have to have faith in faith when we have faith in God.

"Finally, brothers, whatever is true, whatever is noble, whatever is right, whatever is pure, whatever is lovely, whatever is admirable—if anything is excellent or praiseworthy—think about such things. Whatever you have learned or received or heard from me, or seen in me—put it into practice. And the God of peace will be with you" (Phil 4:8-9).

For Individuals or Groups

1. In your own words, summarize the message of the Dragon of Relativism.

2. What effect does the Dragon of Relativism have on faith?

3. How does the Dragon of Relativism open the door for the other Dragons?

4. In what ways do Don Quixote and Willy Loman illustrate the problems of a positive faith (p. 98)?

5. Share ways that you have observed the impact of relative truth or relative morality.

6. The Dragon of Relativism makes us floating islands which occasionally bump into each other. Can you think of instances when relativism has been the culprit isolating you from others? If so, when?

7. How is the Dragon of Relativism active in the faith of a "positive confession"?

8. How does relativism create a vague faith?

9. When has the Dragon of Relativism made you dogmatic or timid (pp. 105-06)?

10. The Scriptures are the foundation of a confident faith. How can we keep in balance the Word and the Spirit to make proper use of the Scriptures?

11. If the Scriptures are God's revealed truth, why do we have so many different Christian denominations and doctrinal positions?

12. Without constant personal study of the Scriptures, we are susceptible to the Dragon of Relativism. Recall a few guidelines mentioned in the chapter that can strengthen your practice of Bible study.

13. How can faith in God equip us with confidence in the face of uncertain or threatening situations?

7
The Dragon of Secularism

Discovering the Pleasure of God's Presence

I glance up and notice a woman dressed in a McDonald's uniform smiling at me as she walks by my table. I am sitting at McDonald's preparing for a workshop on worship. I have a cup of steaming coffee on the table, a warm sweet roll, my Bible and a note pad. I'm tucked away in a corner booth thinking, studying and writing. A few minutes later she is back, cleaning the table around me, lingering over the booth next to mine. I suspect that she wants to talk, so I put down my pen and say hello.

She looks at my Bible and asks, "What are you studying?" I mention something I am learning about worship, but I can feel that she doesn't want to hear me talk. She wants to tell me something. She says she goes to church every week and sings in the choir. But then she gets to the point. She has two children and is about to divorce. Her question: "Where is God in all this?

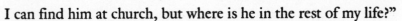
I can find him at church, but where is he in the rest of my life?"

What can I say in the next ten minutes that is going to make a difference in her life? We talk for a few minutes, and then her supervisor comes by to suggest that she wipe some of the tables at the front of the store. Later she comes back with a mop, and we talk a little more. Then it's time for me to go. I walk out in prayerful frustration. What could I have said that would speak to her deep-rooted problems and years of confusion about God?

"Where is God in the rest of my life?" The question rolls around in my head. We are in a struggle of church and state. What is the role of religion in our world? While the issue is being fought out on the battlefields of schools, courts and legislatures, the issue is being fought out in the lives of individuals. The woman at McDonald's is a casualty of the battle; her problem is the daily problem of us all—students, teachers, parents, professionals. What does it mean to know God and what difference does it make on a daily basis?

This problem looms large because we are trapped, culturally and personally in a gigantic battle with the Dragon of Secularism. His creed is, "I am sufficient without God."

This creed is not a blatant declaration of atheism in a philosophy class at a university. It is the creed of men and women in the street, most of whom believe in God. Let me be emphatic. The Dragon of Secularism does not necessarily espouse atheism. In America, only a small percentage of people deny the existence of God. Rather, we are deceived into living without God. The way we approach our lives has little to do with God. The Dragon of Secularism has convinced us that we can handle life on our own. Ironically, we are a secular world full of religious people.

And how do we handle life on our own? Stress, burnout, depression and a list of social ills too numerous to name are symptoms of a people who are overextended, who are over their heads. The bumps and pressures of life put weight on us that we can't carry alone.

A Limiting God

How has the Dragon of Secularism gotten such a hold on our world? He began by convincing us that knowing God restricts us and our freedom. Feuerbach, one of the most influential writers of nineteenth-century Europe said, "There will not be happiness on earth until mankind has been put in the place of God and reason in the place of faith."[1]

The attitude that we are suppressed by God covers the Western world like a fog. Driving on the highway through St. Louis on the way to a football game, I discovered it in a nine-year-old boy. Shortly before I married Jackie, I was housesitting for a family that had gone off for the weekend. As part of the job, I also inherited two boys and three tickets to the Cardinal football game. The older boy knew that I was studying for the ministry and was curious about God. Just off the highway we passed a new church with a modern-looking cross on top—a strange structure that passed for a steeple. When he saw the steeple, he began to question me about my faith. His spiritual hunger was obvious. He asked question after question. Then he hit a wall: "Does believing in God mean that I won't be able to do what I want to do?" I spent a good deal of the football game trying to help him over that objection. He thought God wanted to take away anything enjoyable in his life.

Our fears about God range all the way from the ridiculous ("He will make me be a missionary to Africa" or, "I will have to marry someone who's ugly") to the serious ("I will have to stop padding my expense account" or, "I will need to stop having casual sexual experiences"). God's expectations are real and must be faced. But they are much more difficult to handle because behind the objection is a fear that God will not just limit my actions, but that he will suppress me.

Reaching all the way back to the Fall and the first sin is the implicit assumption that God wouldn't allow Adam and Eve to eat from the tree of good and evil because there was something of great value that he wanted to keep back. Drawing on our natural suspicion of God, the Dragon of Secularism can make a strong cause for living without God. Who wants a God who enjoys inhibiting us?

Likewise, in the field of education, one way or another, students ask me, "What do learning and God have in common?" The answer they expect is, "Not much."

The church is not without blame in this. Whether it is the Medieval church forcing Galileo to recant for teaching that the sun is the center of the solar system or Christians making monkeys out of themselves opposing evolution at the Scopes trial, we have contributed to the common perception that learning and progress are endangered by faith in God.

Consider the *Time* magazine cover story on C. S. Lewis when his book *Miracles* was published in 1947. The author reports that Lewis's popular works espousing Christianity were considered ". . . a kind of academic heresy" by many of his fellow professors.[2] He observes that Lewis's Christianity made him part of a "band of heretics among modern intellectuals: an intellectual that believes in God."[3]

One of the reasons I enjoy ministering in a college arena is because my own experience as a college student was that meeting God made learning come alive for me in a way I never thought possible. I couldn't see how all I was learning fit together until I met the One who made it all. I delight in helping students discover this for themselves. They don't have to put God on the shelf when they walk into a classroom or put their brain on a shelf when they walk into a Bible study. It is a shock to most students, Christian and non-Christian, to learn how historically the Scriptures have been an impetus for learning and for exploring God's world.

Putting a Leash on God

If God limits us, what can we do? The Dragon of Secularism suggests that the answer is to put limits on God. This has been the pattern of Western civilization since the seventeenth century. The Dragon convinces us that progress is made as we "discover" that God has less control and involvement in this world than we previously thought. We believe that science, technology and medicine have progressed to the point where God is not necessary. The great names of the Western world—Rousseau, Voltaire, Darwin, Freud—are those who have charted our current liberation. The modern era can be characterized as the unleashing of mankind and the leashing of God.

The contemporary view of God parallels the fate of monarchies in Europe. God, like royalty, have been reduced to a ceremonial status. We are fascinated by Prince Charles and Di and treat them as celebrities. But we would be much less enamored with them if they had any power. Likewise, we want to have God around as a superstar. We just don't want him to have any authority.

One way we limit God is to redefine him. He is not a person who has opinions and expectations of me. Rather he is energy, the "ground of all being," or the First Cause. To think of God as a person is considered primitive. The "force" in *Star Wars* captures the heart of modern approach. He is energy that is present everywhere that can be used and manipulated by Jedi knights—and those who care to learn how.

Another way we limit God is to distance him. We do not

consider him to be present in the world or concerned with the daily affairs of my life. He is off somewhere running the complex affairs of the universe. We see him as God Emeritus who has retired from day-to-day activity. We keep him in an honorary position and occasionally feel a need to remember him with respect, but know he is really insignificant. The God-is-dead theology of the sixties articulated the logical conclusion of such a position. "We haven't seen him around the world in so long, he must have died. Let's at least be courageous enough to admit it."

A third way we limit God is to localize him. We divide life into secular and religious realms, and then reduce the religious realm to a minor role. A line is drawn between God and the rest of the world. Politics, education, science, medicine, psychology, business are out of bounds for God. He is confined to the church and those who have religious beliefs. What does politics have to do with God? What does working have to do with God? What does school have to do with God? What does parenting have to do with God?

I have read arguments which have dismissed objections to abortion because they were based only on religious convictions. A person's belief in God is not a weighty argument in our world.

When Jimmy Carter was president, he addressed a gathering of business leaders at Disney World. He admonished them to conduct their affairs with a concern for human dignity and basic Christian morality. Critiques following his speech focused on the way he trespassed the line between business and religion— religion and things pertaining to God belong in the church, not in the business world.

A fourth way we limit God is to relativize him. Belief in God is considered a matter of personal choice and optional if you feel a need for this sort of thing. Whatever you think about God for you is fine, and whatever I think about God is fine. God is whatever we want him to be. However we think about him, God serves us, our needs, our wants, rather than us as accountable to him.

With all of our efforts to limit God, we do not want to do away with him completely. We are still fairly religious. God may be limited in our minds. But when our own efforts and the experts fail, he is still there for major problems—death, the loss of a job, the breakup of a marriage . . .

The Dragon of Secularism is not threatened by this. The God we call on for help when all else fails is still a limited God, a God in a box. We take him out of the box when we need help and put him back in once the crisis is over. Or we see God like a repairman that we call when something breaks in our homes. He comes out to us in a white truck, fixes the broken appliance, leaves a bill and drives off again. God's bill is not just for money. Once our life is fixed, we think he wants us to agree to go to church for a period of time or to be nice to others. In the whole exchange there is never a question of fundamental dependence on God. We still see ourselves sufficient for most of life without him.

Secularism in the Church

Active Christians too have been beguiled by the Dragon of Secularism. Large segments of our lives are lived outside the sphere of his care. It is not that we want to. It just never occurs to us to involve him. The spell of this Dragon is so subtly overwhelming that even regular attendance at church and faithful reading of our Bible are not sufficient to protect us.

While in the world the Dragon of Secularism limits God to church and to Sunday, for Christians the Dragon has developed a more sophisticated technique. God is limited to points distributed throughout our day and week. If we are committed to a quiet time, God becomes limited to quiet time. The rest of our day has no conscious intercourse with God. Or if we are committed to a Bible study group, then God only touches us in the Bible study. Or if we are committed to evangelism, then the Dragon would have us believe that only when we evangelize are we doing God's work. In this way our studies at school, or the the account sheet in the office or the kitchen at home are skillfully prevented from becoming constant channels of God's gracious presence with us.

For years I have warned others against separating the secular from the sacred in our lives. Only recently have I made the horrifying discovery that this same split cut my life in two. I have been shocked to realize that I tend to leave God on campus at the end of my day and exclude him from my family. I expect to find him in the times of Bible study, prayer and counseling with students. But in the evening, most of my time at home is overseeing homework assignments, replacing worn-out washers on dripping faucets and chasing boys around the house. I do not naturally expect to see God use these times as avenues for nurturing me and my family. Subconsciously I have felt that we had to get into Bible study and prayer before the family was really doing business with God. In other words, my home life had to look something like my ministry. In new ways I have finally grown to see the "fix it" times, discipline times and play times as God's channel of grace to us. And in new ways we are experiencing God's presence among us.

My own background allowed me to limit God in ways that I was not aware. Each group of Christians has its own way of doing the same thing. Lutherans and Presbyterians can rationalize him—reducing God to and encasing him in a set of propositional truths and theological systems, God becomes someone we encounter only in our doctrine. Charismatics can emotion-alize him—making him into someone we encounter only with our feelings in stimulating worship experiences. Baptists can enshrine him—encountering him only in a past religious experience of walking down an aisle. The evangelical movement of the past fifty or sixty years has frequently personalized and spiritualized God—he was just concerned with saving our souls and getting us into heaven. His lordship did not extend to social and political issues.

In all these ways and more we can limit God. Once we have him defined and placed him in his assigned realm, there is a sense of control. We know what God is supposed to be and how he is supposed to act. We think that we can get on with our life and draw on him when we need him and get around him when it is convenient.

Lynn's eyes were moist. She would glance at me briefly and then quickly look away. I had been speaking to some small group leaders about the difference between having a direct relationship with God as a person instead of a relationship with God just by means of his laws. Lynn came up to me afterward and asked if we could talk. I wasn't able to right then, so we decided to meet in the chapel in a couple of hours.

After we settled down on the carpet at the front of the chapel by the altar rail, Lynn tried to open up, but it was difficult for her. Her face clouded over as soon as she tried to speak. "I'm not sure what I am upset about, but I know it has to do with the way I see God," she said. "I realized that I keep God at a distance. I want to know him, but I don't. It's like Jesus is standing at the door of my life and I have it open just a crack. If I open it all the way, I am sure that he is going to burst in and tell me I have to be a nun. I hope that if I just keep his laws and don't look at him directly, then maybe I can still live my life the way I want to." As we spent an hour in discussion and prayer, Lynn found she was full of guilt because she wanted to be an artist but thought that was not the will of God. Consequently she was living her life as independently of God as she could while still trying to keep him in her life in some way. It was an exhausting balancing act.

I have known people who have faced the painful reality that they were in ministry not from a sense of call but from a sense of guilt. Inevitably they would burnout and despair. In the end they left the ministry. But God redeemed the situation by freeing them to know him and themselves in new ways.

Sometimes it doesn't always work out that way. The president of one Inter-Varsity chapter discovered that she was involved in Christian leadership because she didn't think the rest of campus life—student government, sororities, service clubs—was an option. She developed a resentment toward me and God because she felt we were forcing her to do things her heart was not in.

The church, like the world, acts as though a deep relationship with God limits our lives. Since God is concerned only with the religious, commitment to God means going into some type of full-time Christian work, becoming a minister or a missionary. To become a painter or a politician or an accountant is not a kosher option. This creates intense stress. To cope we keep God at a distance or try to conform by limiting ourselves.

Our measures of spirituality are so feeble. If we are barely committed to God, then we attend services once a week. If we have a solid commitment, we go twice a week. If we are really committed, then we go three times a week. And if we have any interest beyond that, we can get involved in committees and visitation. Is it any wonder that people show up at a church for a period of a couple of years, become heavily involved and then drop out again?

We pray before we start on a project to dedicate it to him, and we pray in gratitude once it is finished. But it never occurs to us that God is involved in the entire project and that we should be in a dialog with God all the way through. Fervent prayer and a sense of dependence on God arise only if something goes wrong. "The only thing left to do is pray."

The Dragon of Secularism puts God in a box. When we give ourselves over to God, instead of letting him out of the box, we try to climb inside. So of course we feel oppressed and confined. What we need is a bigger view of God that will allow us a bigger view of ourselves and give us room to live in his world. There is plenty of freedom in God's world; freedom to learn and study all kinds of academic disciplines, freedom to be creative as an actor, painter or poet; freedom to go into business and earn money. But first we must transform our understanding of the secular-sacred dichotomy that restricts God.

Taming the Dragon of Secularism

We may know all about God, but the way of secularism prevents us from knowing God. If we are to escape secularism we must discover a view of God that is big enough to cover all areas of life. And we must rediscover that we are creatures of the ever-present Creator—always and in all areas dependent; never sufficient for life without him.

A broader understanding of God begins in the first chapters of Genesis and the creation story. But even more than being a story about creation, it is a story about the Creator. As I glance through the first chapter I see God mentioned in verse after verse. God said. God saw. God called. God made. God placed. God created. God is more than a distant being standing off in space speaking a world into existence and then stepping back to see how it unfolds. He is intimately involved. He carefully develops his world a day at a time. And at the end of every creation day he is present to evaluate the results and pronounce them good. In chapter 2 the focus sharpens specifically to mankind. God is so intimately involved with Adam that he notices Adam's loneliness and creates Eve as a companion. As we read about the sin of Adam and Eve in chapter 3 we get the impression that God was in the habit of a daily visit.

Even after the Fall, this picture of God as present never changes throughout the Scriptures. God carried on a dialog with Cain prior to Cain's murder of Abel. Even after Cain's sin God is not silent. He personally delivers the judgment. In the face of disobedience and degeneration of the race, God was present and spoke to Noah. Abraham, the Patriarchs, the Judges, the Prophets—their experience displays that God is as present and involved in the ongoing history of the world as he was in his initial creation.

God's presence is the central issue of biblical faith. Nowhere is this more clearly seen in the Old Testament than in Moses' dialog with God on Mount Sinai. Moses says to God, "If your Presence does not go with us, do not send us up from here. . . . What else will distinguish me and your people from all the other people on the face of the earth?" (Ex 33:15-16).

In the New Testament, when Jesus was born, he was to be called Immanuel—God with us (Mt 1:23). And Jesus' promise to the disciples just before his ascension is, "I will be with you always" (Mt 28:20).

The great leaders of the church have continued to proclaim that God is present in his world. Some were great theologians like Augustine or Calvin who sought to understand life in light of the presence of God. Some were devotional masters like St. Anthony or Bernard of Clairvaux who taught ways to worship him. Some were great preachers and evangelists who appealed to masses like George Whitefield or John Wesley.

One of the greatest witnesses to God's presence was never a leader at all, only a cook's helper. Nicolas Hermon in seventeenth-century France (popularly known as Brother Lawrence) displayed a remarkable and serene faith that God was present with him throughout his day. He would often begin his day with this prayer, "O my God, you are always with me. Since I must now, in obedience to your will for me, apply my mind to my day's work, grant me the grace I shall need to continue through it in your presence."[4]

Sacred Lord

God is with us at all times. But there is a sense in which he is different and separate. Words like *holy, sacred, consecrate,* and *sanctify* are part and parcel of biblical faith. Implicit in these words is the concept of separation and limitation, something or someone being set aside from common everyday use. God's holiness makes his presence an uncommon experience. We can't take him for granted.

When Moses encountered God at the burning bush he was commanded, "Do not come any closer. . . . Take off your sandals, for the place where you are standing is holy ground" (Ex 3:5). God was present in the burning bush in a special way, and Moses was required to be humbly respectful.

When God chooses to reveal himself to the nation of Israel at Mt. Sinai after their deliverance from Egypt, God again sets up limits. "The people cannot come up to Mount Sinai because you yourself warned us, 'Put limits for the people around the mountain and set it apart as holy' " (Ex 19:23). After the people had spent three days in consecrating themselves God manifests himself in smoke and lightning and speaks to Moses in front of the entire nation.

If God is present in his world, then how does the idea of holiness—separation and limitation—fit in? All which is called holy is intended as the means not by which God is quarantined, but as a channel through which God reveals himself to us. Did God need a sound-and-light show in the form of the burning bush or flaming mountaintop? Obviously not. He spoke to Elijah in a still, small voice. Is God restricted to certain places with set boundaries by which he can reveal himself? Again the answer is no: "The heavens declare the glory of God" (Ps 19:1).

It is through the holy, that which is set apart, that we are assisted in being with God in all his world. The experience of the holy focuses our thoughts, clears our minds and makes us receptive.

The burning bush got Moses' attention, the smoking mountain the attention of Israel. The majesty and might of God which is present everywhere was displayed to Moses and Israel so that it could be seen.

We all need the experience of the holy if we are live with God in all our lives—holy things, people and places are God's gifts to us. I recognize God in all areas of my life because I can read his holy book. I am strengthened to live the entire week with him because he has set aside one day in seven to be devoted to rest and worship. I can find help and strength through holy people (though they don't wear long robes or hair shirts). They are ordinary people who have been set aside to devote their time and energy to prayer, study, worship and ministry.

I believe that we can set up holy times and places in our lives through which God chooses to meet us. The beach at sunset or a table in a shopping mall in the afternoons are both places and times where I have been privileged to discover more of God's presence. Whether it is a dorm room desk in the morning before classes or the dining room table before others get up, if we set aside the time and place, God will make it a holy place.

While God meets us in holiness, he is, of course, not restricted to his holy book. Wonderful things about God can be discovered on the pages of many others. (I love the Chronicles of Narnia for this reason.) Nor is God restricted to Sunday as his holy day, nor to ministers as holy people, nor to a quiet time as the only time with God. We are back again at a dynamic tension which we must keep in balance.

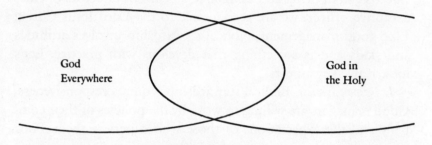

Figure 11. God Everywhere and God in the Holy

If we emphasize either one too strongly we end up outside of biblical truth and healthy Christian experience.

Stewardship
We experience this tension in our accountability to God. "Be holy as I am holy" is a theme running throughout the Scriptures. To be near God is to know that I must obey him. And somehow the Dragon of Secularism tugs at my mind so that I, like the nine-year-old in St. Louis or the student who wanted to be an artist, have a habit of thinking that accountability means inhibition. If I get close to God, then I can't be what I want to be or do what I want to do.

But in Christ, accountability to God is not intended to enhance rather than to inhibit. In Genesis it is clear that we are created to be lords of the earth, stewards of the Creator to rule the creatures, be fruitful and cultivate the earth. Accountability to God means opportunity. We are privileged as creatures made in God's image to be responsible to God for his world.

Thus stewardship is the discipline by which we practice accountability to God. Stewardship strikes at the root of secularism. It is a biblical term, similar to our concept of management. But instead of being accountable to a board of directors or chief executive officer, we are accountable to the Lord Jesus Christ. Like good management, biblical stewardship involves attitudes and skills and is something that develops with practice. Let's look at five key aspects.

1. Responsiveness. Biblical stewardship requires responsiveness. Good managers are willing to work by the policies of their company and the expectations of those who supervise them. Poor managers set their own agendas while ignoring directions from above.

Responsiveness is more than just discovering what God wants me to do in life, such as be a lawyer, teacher or electrician . . . It is a way of life. It is living with a cocked ear to the God who is with us. "I will instruct you and teach you in the way you should go; I will counsel you and watch over you. Do not be like the horse or the mule, which have no understanding but must be controlled by bit and bridle or they will not come to you" (Ps 32: 8-9).

A spiritual revolution occurred in my life when I discovered how unresponsive I was to God. In the early stages of working on this book I had a strong sense that I needed to stop the background research and get on with the writing. (The first draft of the activism chapter had fifty-one footnotes.) I felt strongly that this was the Lord urging me, but it was in a direction in which I didn't want to go. I remember slamming a book shut and stomping out of the library. If I couldn't do the research I needed to, then I would not be able to write well. I remember looking up at the sky and asking in an accusing tone, "Do you want me to write a lousy book?"

Over the next months as I struggled with my own desires, quiet spiritual urges and interaction with others, I became convinced that God was in fact guiding me. Andy, my editor, suggested that I redirect my efforts from research to writing!

While I considered myself to be someone who was seeking God's will, I wasn't really open to it if it was different from my own desires. Soon I noticed how an attitude of unresponsiveness filled my life. Our wills and emotions are bound by a habit of resisting. Each resistance binds us a little more. If we are to be free, then step by step we must practice following God's lead. Over the last couple of years God has been continually guiding me past a resistant spirit.

For most of us, the quality of our life with God goes up and down with our responsiveness quotient. There is less anger and more intimacy with God and others when we are responsive. With friends or family or coworkers, God is always placing us in situations that require us to grow and change. We all would prefer to keep things the way they are. But in the practice of responsiveness we discover new wisdom and effectiveness.

2. Initiative. Biblical stewardship also requires initiative. God expects us to get on with the task of obeying him and cultivating the world he has entrusted to us. Responsiveness is not passiveness. To confuse the two can be spiritually fatal.

In Jesus' parable of the talents a man goes on a journey and entrusts his stewards with money: "To one he gave five talents of money, to another two talents, and to another one talent, each according to his ability" (Mt 25:15). The man going on the journey gives no instructions on how the money is to be used, just that they were responsible for it. When the man returns he discovers that two stewards invested their money and doubled it while one steward buried the money and made nothing. Two stewards took initiative. One steward was passive. The two are affirmed. The one rebuked.

Good executives do not need someone always checking up on them to see if they are doing the job. Once they know what is expected and to whom they are accountable, they expect to use their skills, ingenuity and energy to accomplish the task. This is similar to what God wants of us. If you are a student, you don't need to wonder whether it is God's will for you to study. (This comes as a shock to some.) If you are a father, you don't need to wonder if it is God's will for you to care for your family. If you are in business, you don't need to wonder if it is God's will for you to provide a quality product at a fair price.

A good steward practices responsive initiative.

3. Resources. Closely tied to initiative are resources—as the parable of the talents illustrates. God has entrusted to us what we need to live in the world. We are to make the most of it. We are held accountable by God to grow and develop to the fullest extent possible! He does not inhibit us.

Biblical stewardship requires wise use of resources. Just as a good manager knows resources of people, money and time that he has been assigned, the way we live must include a wise understanding and use of God's gifts of our energy level, time, abilities, spiritual gifts, friends, money and possessions.

I am typing this book on a computer. I have no technical background in data processing. The only thing I know is how to turn on the machine and use the word-processing program. But the computer has the ability to keep a mailing list, send electronic mail, keep my business accounts in order and do many other things I haven't even thought of yet. So I have promised myself that after I finish this book I will spend time exploring its capabilities. In a similiar way, we have been given so much from God that needs to be discovered, explored, developed and employed. All our lives we can look forward to greater use of the resources that God has given to us.

Wise stewardship of resources is a continual battle. As we've seen in earlier chapters, it is all to easy to become overextended. And it is just as easy to justify it in the name of serving God. Recently I found myself pinched between too many commitments and not enough time (activism again). The result—doing lots of things poorly and even overlooking a few promises. When this led to a conflict with my wife, Jackie, at home, I went for a long drive on a country road. Eventually I pulled over at a roadside park overlooking a lake. I strode up and down the shore telling God that I was angry for not being appreciated. Besides that, I let him know that he wasn't managing my life very well at all, thank you. Everything I was doing in the name of ministry seemed to be getting me into trouble. In the midst of my little tantrum, it began to dawn on me that the problem was mine and not God's. I had been a poor steward of my time and energy.

If we are to live as biblical stewards, we must take inventory. "Know thyself" is good advice. We may find that we are living beyond our resources, or we may find that we have gifts and abilities we are not using and need to put to work. It is false humility to ignore these.

The issue is crucial for students or those in midlife. When you find yourself at a decision point about career, chances are good that God is leading you in ways that will satisfy your interests and allow your abilities to be expressed. To live to the fullest, we must pay attention to ourselves.

4. *Quality.* Biblical stewardship requires quality. We should

seek to be the best that we can be. We are to strive for excellence. "Whatever you do, whether in word or deed, do it all in the name of the Lord Jesus, giving thanks to God the Father through him" (Col 3:17).

I have enjoyed the emphasis on excellence in management literature. For the book *In Search of Excellence*, the authors conducted a study of successful corporations to see what they were doing right. They discovered that more than an emphasis on profits or quantity was a concern to be the best in their field. The people in those corporations, from top to bottom, worked hard because they had a sense of pride and participation in a quality organization. How much more should we, children of God, take pride to do the very best we can because we serve our Creator-Redeemer!

Look at your work, your relationships, all of your life. Work not for success, but to live well in all things. The greatest motivation in life is what we may hear at its end when our Lord pronounces, "Well done, good and faithful servant."

5. *Communication.* Finally, biblical stewardship requires communication—prayer. Good managers make frequent reports to their supervisors, keeping them appraised of the progress of the project. Often we don't know what to say to God in prayer because we think it has to deal with church or a major crisis. Let's break prayer out its "religious box." Why shouldn't we talk over the events of our lives with the one to whom we are accountable?

I experienced a revolution when I discovered that prayer was a way to report to the Lord on the progress of my life. Much of my prayers used to center on telling God what I thought he should do to help me and the people I was concerned about. Now I lay concerns before him as a steward discusses the problems incurred in management. "Here is what is going on and I am concerned, Lord. What do you think?" Repeatedly I find new insights and fresh courage from those times of prayer.

Tell God about the progress of your studies. Tell him about your frustrations and fears. Speak to God about your spouse and tell him what's going on in your marriage. Give God a report on your job, what you enjoy and what you are anxious about. Don't always tell him what to do about your concerns. Instead try asking him what he thinks about your situation. You will find perspective you didn't expect.

Stewardship requires that we live with right values. We live not for money but to please the Lord. We work not for a need to produce but from a sense of divine accountability. We live not from our own resources but in dependence on our God. We work not to impress others but to express ourselves. We believe not because it will make us successful but because we know it is what God requires. We live all of life in the presence of the holy God who directs us. Stewardship, rightly understood, becomes an expression of health and a way to tame all the Dragons.

Emotional about God

Taming the Dragon of Secularism should lead us to experience God as a way of life.

We need not be afraid of this. On the contrary, we should expect that knowing God will be a constant and expanding experience. Some Christians have avoided feelings because "they are not dependable, and besides, our world is so experience-oriented." Certainly our relationship to God must not be dependent on emotions, but there is something wrong if they are absent.

There is an art gallery in Jackson that I love to visit. The gallery handles artists who paint in the tradition of Monet. Every painting is filled with light and air. It doesn't matter whether they paint a field or river, a house or people, their work shimmers with energy. Whenever I am on that side of town I make a visit to drink in their vision and skill. I marvel at how they could capture such beauty on canvas. I appreciate their technique, but I am not an educated art lover. I just know I like their work. For me to enjoy the paintings is a wonderful experience.

We should experience our God in the same way. We don't have to be skilled theologians or professional churchgoers to enjoy his handiwork. We live in his world and are immersed in his presence. We need only look past the filters the Dragons have placed over our minds. As one poet wrote, "The world is charged with the grandeur of God."[5]

When a man and woman marry, they commit themselves to staying together regardless of how they feel. But if they don't have romantic feelings as a part of their marriage, then something is wrong. The solution is not to dissolve the union but to begin to ask what is blocking the feelings. Then they will want to take steps to remedy the situation. I am convinced that secularism and the rest of the Dragons are major blocks to our experience of God.

In 1746 Jonathan Edwards wrote that Christians should have an experiental knowledge of religion, "a sense of the heart, wherein the mind not only speculates and beholds, but relishes and feels."[6]

How can we know the presence of God who is with us in love and not be moved to love in return? Edwards writes, "True religion which God requires . . . does not consist in weak and lifeless inclinations, raised but a little above the state of indifference."[7] He asks, "Who will deny that true religion consists [in] the fervent exercises of the heart."[8]

We experience God in worship, not in a worship limited to

How We See Secularism

Secularism wants me to believe:	"I am sufficient without God."
How secularism is seen in the world:	Limited God, limiting God
How secularism is seen in the church:	Sunday only, church only

How We Defeat Secularism

The biblical value to combat secularism:	Creation—"God is present with me."
The spiritual discipline to combat secularism:	Stewardship
The result of defeating secularism:	Experience

Figure 12. Defeating Secularism

Sunday and a church building, but in a worship that fills our week. Worship is an experience with God that comes from all of life. Hugs of greeting from my wife and boys at the end of the day fill me with gratitude for God's goodness to me. Drives on country roads as seasons change draw forth an appreciation of God's skill and creativity. Times of depression and sadness make me look forward to the Lord's return when this out-of-kilter world is set straight again.

Everything in life, every experience can be a sacrament taking us to the One who is the source of all experience. The devotional life is not just the time I spend with God in front of my Bible but a way of living all day long.

"Thou, O Lord my God, art above all things the best; Thou alone art most high, Thou alone most powerful, Thou alone most sufficient and most full, Thou alone most sweet and most full of consolation, Thou alone art most lovely and loving, Thou alone most noble and glorious above all things; in whom all good things together both perfectly are, and ever have been and shall be. That therefore it is too small and unsatisfying, whatever Thou bestowest on me besides Thyself, . . . whilst Thou are not seen, nor fully obtained. For surely my heart cannot truly rest, nor be entirely contended unless it rest in Thee, and surmount all gifts and every creature."⁹

For Individuals or Groups

1. Because of the influence of secularism, we see God as a limiting God. What are a couple of ways we believe that God limits us?

2. Because we fear being limited by God, we in turn seek to limit God. What are a few of the ways that we seek to put a leash on him?

3. Secularism in America is not the same thing as atheism. We still need him for special occasions. In what ways do we keep God around as a God of last resort?

4. One of the ways that the Dragon of Secularism invades the church is by localizing God. What are some of the ways that we limit him to specific points in our lives?

5. The presence of God is the central issue of biblical faith. How do the Scriptures help us to see God involved in every area of life?

6. The holiness of God means that he is separate from the world. How can he be holy and present at the same time?

7. How does biblical stewardship mean opportunity rather than inhibition?

8. Recall several aspects of biblical stewardship (pp. 131-37). Which do you see already present in your life? Which do you see a need to work on?

9. How are responsiveness to God and personal initiative both necessary for balanced stewardship?

10. In what ways can stewardship become an expression of health and a way to defeat all the Dragons?

11. Knowing God should be more than intellectual knowledge. It should be an experience. In what one new area of your life can you experience the living God this week?

8
Being a Dragon Slayer

We have looked at six Dragons and considered a way to face each one. Most of you will have discovered a gruesome dragon pet or two which seems to have an especially strong hold on you. But Dragons work as a band. When you see one you should know that others are present as well, lurking in the shadows. Defining the agenda for this world in which we live, the Dragons are an interlocking value system, and they invade as a diabolical legion.

Materialism requires activism as a means to accumulation and affluence.

Materialism and activism together convince us that the resources to work hard and become wealthy are within us, and so we fall prey to individualism.

But since individualism leaves us feeling drained and lonely, we turn to others and seek to extract recognition and approval by conforming to the expectations of others.

When all the immense effort required by the Dragons begins to leave us feeling exhausted, the Dragon of Relativism waits in hiding to tell us that we can be and do anything the other Dragons suggest—if only we believe.

Lurking behind them all, providing the power of their scorching lies, is the Dragon of Secularism telling us that we are sufficient without God.

The Dragons of the World are not choosy about which one dominates us. Perhaps it is individualism. Focusing on ourselves, we are easily driven to activism to prove that we are valuable.

Or perhaps secularism dominates our lives. Once we believe we are sufficient without God, it is inevitable that we will become individualistic. We will look inside ourselves for a sense of significance.

Or perhaps we are beguiled by relativism. Once we believe that we are whatever we believe, then there is little need for God. But without God we have a void in our lives which we will seek to fill by listening to the Dragon of Conformism.

A Comprehensive Battle Plan

After giving a talk on the Dragons at a meeting of ministers, I happened to notice the notes of one of the pastors summarizing my talk. He had written, "Conformed, deformed, informed, transformed." The Dragons conform us to the world, and then deform us. If we are to escape them we must become informed and transformed.

The Dragons have conformed us. They are the power of the world. They define our aspirations and desires, telling us what is worthwhile and what we must do to be worthwhile. If we are to make it in the world, then we must conform to their agenda.

The values of my country, my friends, my associates and even my family—these naturally are my values as well.

In the process of conforming us, the Dragons deform us. The Dragons of the World are not just "out there." They are the mental habits which shape our minds and hearts. The values of God which give value to our lives become misshapen beyond recognition.

Once during a group discussion on the Dragons, I noticed that the whole tenor of the discussion was hostile. People were angry at the way they perceived the Dragons forcing them into a mold of worldliness. They wanted to erect walls around their lives and their church. However, in further discussion with people it became clear to us all that the Dragons of the World have become the Dragons of the Mind. They are inside us.

Since we can never erect walls to keep the Dragons out, we must choose another line of defense. We must understand them—what they are and how they work. When we see them operate within our lives, as they will always be on this side of heaven, then we can bring them to God. You see, to defeat the Dragons of the World we do not eradicate them. Rather we bring them to the One who can transform our hearts.

God's Deliverance

C. S. Lewis in *The Voyage of the Dawn Treader* tells the story of a boy who is turned into a dragon. Eustice Scrubb was an extremely unpleasant boy, self-centered and insufferable. He and several of his friends end up in an adventure in the magical land of Narnia. Embarking on a voyage to find several Dukes and Lords of Narnia, the ship Dawn Treader stops at some fascinating islands.

On one of the islands Eustice slips away and discovers a dragon's den filled with treasure. He climbs down in the den, and begins to load his pockets with diamonds and slips a jewel-studded bracelet on his arm. After being down there awhile, and being tired from his adventure, he falls asleep.

When Eustice wakes up from his nap, he discovers to his horror that he has turned into a dragon. "Sleeping on a dragon's hoard with greedy, dragonish thoughts in his heart, he had become a dragon himself."

Eustice was terrified. He makes several attempts to get help from his friends, but there is nothing they can do. Feeling terribly alone he crawls off in the woods in despair, fearing that he is condemned to spend the rest of his life as a dragon.

Then Aslan the lion appears to Eustice and tells him to undress. At first he is confused. After all, he wasn't wearing any clothes. But then he reasons that since a dragon is similar to a snake, perhaps he can shed his skin. As he scratches himself with his dragon claws, scales start falling off. Before long, he steps out of his skin rejoicing to think that he had been delivered.

But then, to his dismay, he discovers that he is still a dragon. So he starts scratching again and peels off another suit of skin. And again Eustice discovers that he is still a dragon. So a third time Eustice works to shed his skin and still he is a dragon.

At this point Aslan speaks, "You will have to let me undress you." With his huge claws Aslan makes a tear so deep that it seems to go to Eustice's heart. And as a thick, dark layer of skin is pealed away, he becomes a boy again.

God must deliver us as Aslan delivered Eustice Scrubb. Only he can deliver us from hearts deformed and conformed by the Dragons. If we seek to defeat the Dragons of the World by our own efforts and determination, we place ourselves more deeply in their clutches. They will grow in power fueled by our self-generated focus on them. Our only hope is to cast ourselves on God.

Repentance

While God must deliver us from the Dragons of the World that have invaded our hearts, there is something we can and must do. We must repent.

Repentance is not just a one-time act which takes place at the point of conversion. Repentance must be a way of life as we battle the Dragons. For several years I read the Sermon on the Mount daily. Time after time I discovered that I could not meet Jesus' standard as I measured myself against the demands of the inner righteousness of the Sermon. Each morning as I came to him I found myself embarrassed. "Lord, I have done it again." Daily I had to repent.

If we intend to defeat the Dragons, then we must struggle with them. Activists, such as myself, will have to repent frequently, more than once a day. I may have my perspective right in the morning as I sit down at my desk, but by lunch I am functioning as a driven person whose sense of identity depends on what happens in the next phone calls I make.

Those of us who are preoccupied with owning and buying in order to establish our sense of value will find that our spiritual side of life is repeatedly slipping into the background. Those of us possessed by the Dragon of Conformism will find that despite the best intentions, we will attempt to paint impressive pictures about our actions and achievements the minute we meet another person.

As I began to practice daily repentance I discovered two things. First, I discovered the Lord's graciousness. Time after time, as I repented I discovered a growing sense of the Lord's forgiveness. Second, I began to discover little victories. For instance, over a period of time, as I caught judgment of others in my heart (Mt 7:1-5) and repented, I discovered that a judgmental attitude no longer controlled me as intensely as it used to do.

Gradually, under the grace of God, we will begin to reshape our dragonish mental habits.

As I struggled with repentance I discovered that, coming from God, *repentance* is not a word of condemnation but a gracious offer of freedom. Imagine a king who happens to go for a stroll in his kingdom one day and sees one of his subjects about to be hanged. He inquires into the man's offense, thinks for a moment, and then turns to the condemned man who is standing on the gallows with a rope around his neck. He speaks a word of reprieve. "Repent." The criminal has been offered a second chance. If he does repent, he can take the rope from his neck, come down off the platform and go on with his life.

This is the essence of our battle with the Dragons. God must deliver us, but we must repent. If we slip to one pole or the other, we fall back into the clutches of the Dragons. But in the balance we grow and begin to live by the values of God.

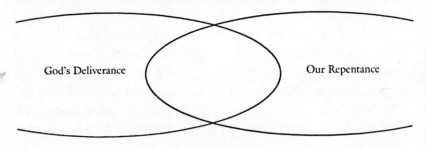

Figure 13. Deliverance and Repentance

God's Value System
Just as the Dragons of the World are a value system, God's values are a system too. When one value begins to be transformed in our hearts, others will follow. As I begin to desire the *spiritual side of reality* I begin to glimpse *responsibility* as some-

thing more than actions and results. There is a new way of seeing God as the one who takes action in my life and a freedom to see myself as a responder to his initiatives. Once I begin to value *relationships* I find I am free to enjoy my own sense of *individuality*. And once I understand that faith is built upon the *revelation* of the One who shows himself to me, I am free to see God *present* with me and glorified in all his creation.

As godly values begin to be transformed in our hearts, we should expect to see godly results. *Faith* that is alive will provide us with a *peace* which puts our eccentric lives in order. *Intimacy* with others will lead to a *inner contentment*. A settled *confidence* in God will free us to look for the *experience of a heart devotion* throughout our weeks and years with God.

We need to practice Christian disciplines if we are to defeat the Dragons. As you look at the chart on page 148, the disciplines are the column between God's values and godly results. While Christian disciplines are not the source of values nor the granter of results, they are a means of God's grace to us.

Heart disease is a major killer. A primary cause of heart disease is cholesterol in the blood vessels. As the vessels become clogged, they lose their ability to convey blood to and from the heart. Many cardiologists believe that exercise is a means of preventing the accumulation in the veins and of reducing the build-up if it has already begun.

There is a spiritual analogy here. As we practice the disciplines, we discover that our hearts become healthy and vital with spiritual life.

The Adventure

I am excited about the adventure that lies before us. We are privileged to be God's people in his world at an opportune time. While the structures of the world are breaking down and the

How We See the Dragons of the World

The Dragons	The World	The Church
Materialism I am what I own.	Accumulation Affluence	Prosperity Apathy
Activism I am what I do. I am what I produce.	Consuming careers	Consuming ministry
Individualism I am the source of my own value.	Liberated loneliness	Christian loneliness
Conformism I am who others recognize me to be.	Perpetual public relations	Spiritual public relations
Relativism I am whatever I want to believe.	Positive thinking Uncertain truth	Positive faith Uncertain faith
Secularism I am sufficient without God.	Limited God Limiting God	Sunday only Church only

How We Defeat the Dragons of the World

Biblical Value	Discipline	Result
Spirituality God's Spirit is in me.	Meditation	Faith
Responsibility God makes me fruitful.	Dialogical prayer	Peace
Relationships God made us in his image.	Community	Intimacy
Individuality God knows me.	Solitude	Contentment
Revelation God shows himself to me.	Bible study	Confidence
Creation God is present with me.	Stewardship	Experience

Figure 14. Defeating the Dragons of the World

means of transmitting traditional values are slipping away, we as Christians have something to say. Instead of only lamenting the decay of the world, we can go on to build up the church. We can pursue God and enjoy him.

The character of the church is the crucial issue. Let nothing distract us from this. Paul admonished Timothy, "Watch your life and doctrine closely. Persevere in them, because if you do, you will save both yourself and your hearers" (1 Tim 4:16). What was true for Timothy on a personal scale is true for the church on a corporate scale.

I am not suggesting that we ignore the world, nor that we have no responsibility to affect it. But if we change ourselves first, we will have a transforming effect on the world around us.

When God determined to destroy Sodom and Gomorrah, he first consulted with Abraham. Abraham appealed to God for mercy, and God agreed not to destroy the cities if only ten righteous people could be discovered there. But they were not found, and the cities were destroyed. The lesson for us? It is not how wicked our world is but how righteous we are.

I am not one to look back on the early church as a golden age to which we must return. They had their problems and struggles just as we do. But I was challenged by a recent article in the *Evangelical Newsletter* on the character of the early church and its effect on the world in which it lived.

T. R. Glover has said, " 'The early Christian church conquered because the Christians of those days out-thought, out-lived and out-died the pagans.' . . . For them power meant being filled with the Holy Spirit; privilege implied becoming a twice born child of God; prestige connoted being one in Christian fellowship. As for wealth, it was rare—and when present it was shared.

"Although faith was intense, 'name-it-and-claim it' theology—focusing on this world's good and success—did not exist. Psychological 'carrots' were not used by a minister to bait people into the kingdom. Listeners were candidly instructed to count the cost."[1]

We are to be God's people in the world. Will we outlive those around us who don't know God and who do not yet belong to his people?

Inside and outside the church there is a great lamentation over the loss of values. What is right? What is wrong? What is worthwhile? What is not? What makes a person feel good and significant? We have the opportunity to demonstrate that there are answers. For the sake of the church and the sake of the culture, we must exercise discernment, understanding what it means to be in the world, but not of it. Let us not be conformed to the world but be transformed by the renewing of our minds.

It is the only way to tame the Dragons of the World.

For Individuals or Groups

1. We all have our own pet Dragons. Which Dragons do you think are most active in your life?

2. While some Dragons may have a stronger influence on us than others, they function together as a value system. How do they work together?

3. Explain how one Dragon opens the way to the rest.

4. Why is is not possible to erect walls to keep the Dragons out of the church and out of our lives?

5. What does the story of Eustice Scrubb, the boy who became a dragon, have to teach us about defeating the Dragons?

6. God's call to repent is not a word of condemnation but of liberation. Why is the lifestyle of repentance necessary for Dragon slaying?

7. Just as the Dragons are a value system, godly values are a system also. How are they inter-related?

8. What results should we expect in our lives when we are living according to the value of God?

9. Describe how the disciplines are a channel between godly values and godly results in our lives?

10. Why is the character of the Church the crucial issue in this time of values decay which has produced the Dragons?

11. What differences do you expect to see in your life as a result of your study of *Defeating the Dragons of the World?*

Notes

Chapter 1: Discovering the Deforming Dragons
[1]George Gallup, Jr., and David Poling, *The Search for America's Faith* (Nashville: Abingdon, 1980), p. 174.
[2]Jack Kent, *There Are No Such Things As Dragons* (New York: Golden Press, 1975).
[3]Eugene Peterson, *A Long Obedience in the Same Direction* (Downers Grove, Ill.: InterVarsity Press, 1980), p. 11.

Chapter 2: The Dragon of Materialism
[1]Carl Sagan, *Cosmos* (New York: Random House, 1980), p. 4.
[2]Ronald J. Sider, *Rich Christians in an Age of Hunger* (Downers Grove, Ill.: InterVarsity Press, 1977), p. 46.
[3]Gail Sheehy, *Pathfinders* (New York: Bantam Books, 1981), p. 55.
[4]Gloria Copeland, *God's Will Is Prosperity* (Tulsa, Okla.: Harrison House, 1978), p. 46.
[5]Os Guinness, *The Gravedigger File* (Downers Grove, Ill.: InterVarsity Press, 1983), p. 132.
[6]Bernard of Clairvaux, "On the Love of God," in *Late Medieval Mysticism*, ed. Ray Petry (Philadelphia: Westminster, 1957), p. 59.
[7]William Perkins, "A Treatise on the Vocations and Callings of Men" in *The Courtenay Library of Reformation Classics*, ed. George Yule (Berkshire, England, 1970), p. 464.
[8]C. Stacey Woods, *Some Ways of God* (Downers Grove, Ill.: InterVarsity Press, 1975), p. 86.
[9]Morton Kelsey, *Encounter with God* (Minneapolis: Bethany 1972), p. 58.
[10]J. I. Packer, *Knowing God* (Downers Grove, Ill.: InterVarsity Press, 1973), p. 19.

Chapter 3: The Dragon of Activism
[1]Cotton Mather, quoted in *The American Idea of Success* by Richard Huber (New York: McGraw Hill, 1971), p. 13.
[2]Martin Luther, quoted by Leland Ryken in "Puritan Work Ethic: The Dignity of Life's Labor," *Christianity Today*, 19 October 1979, p. 17.
[3]Jacques Ellul, *Prayer and Modern Man* (New York: Seabury Press, 1979), p. vi.

[4]Ibid., pp. 143-44.
[5]Richard Foster, *Celebration of Discipline* (San Francisco: Harper and Row, 1978), p. 33.
[6]John White, *Daring to Draw Near* (Downers Grove, Ill.: InterVarsity Press, 1977), p. 14.
[7]Martin Luther, cited in Donald Bloesch, *The Struggle of Prayer* (New York: Harper & Row, 1980), p. 63.
[8]Andrew Murray, *The Ministry of Intercession* (Old Tappan, N.J.: Fleming H. Revell), p. 83.

Chapter 4: The Dragon of Individualism
[1]Robert Ringer, *Looking Out For Number One* (New York: Fawcett, 1977), p. 12.
[2]Shirley MacLaine, *Washington Post* Interview, 1977.
[3]Robert N. Bellah, Richard Madsen et al., *Habits of the Heart:Individualism and Commitment in American Life* (New York: Harper and Row, 1985), p. 23.
[4]Ibid., p. 16.
[5]Neil Diamond, " 'I Am,' I Said" (Los Angeles: Prophet Music, 1971).
[6]A.W. Tozer, *The Knowledge of the Holy* (New York: Harper and Row, 1961), p. 9.
[7]Thomas à Kempis, *The Imitation of Christ* (Chicago: Moody Press, 1958), p. 112.

Chapter 5: The Dragon of Conformism
[1]Bellah et al., *Habits of the Heart*, p. 48.
[2]Johan C. Harvey with Cynthia Katz, *If I Am So Successful, Why Do I Feel Like a Fake? The Imposter Phenomenon* (New York: St. Martin's Press, 1985), p. 3.
[3]"The Sayings of the Fathers," in *Western Asceticism*, ed. Owen Chadwick (Philadelphia: Westminster, 1957), p. 101.
[4]Richard Rolle, "The Mending of Life" in *Late Medieval Mysticism*, ed. Ray C. Petry (Philadelphia: Westminster, 1957), p. 235.

Chapter 6: The Dragon of Relativism
[1]Napolean Hill, *Think and Grow Rich* (Hollywood, Calif.: Wilshire Book Company, 1966), p. 51.
[2]Printice Mulford, quoted by Richard Heber in *The American Idea of Success* (New York: McGraw Hill, 1971), p. 126.
[3]Coué, quoted by Richard Heber, *The American Idea of Success*, p. 181.
[4]Robert Ringer, *Looking Out for Number One* (New York: Fawcett Crest, 1977), p. 8.
[5]In *God's Will Is Prosperity*, Gloria Copeland writes, "God is allowing whatever you allow! He has given you authority, and according to His Word, you can have what you say," p. 80.
[6]Conferences of Cassian, *Western Asceticism*, ed. Owen Chadwick (Philadelphia: Westminster, 1957), p. 245.

Chapter 7: The Dragon of Secularism
[1]Ludwig Feuerbach, quoted by William L. Langer in *Perspectives in Western Civilization, Vol.11: Political and Social Upheaval in the Nineteenth Century* (New York: Harper and Row, 1972), p. 517.

[2]*Time*, 8 September 1947, p. 65.

[3]Ibid., p. 65.

[4]Brother Lawrence, *Closer Than a Brother*, ed. David Winter (Carol Stream, Ill.: Harold Shaw Publishers, 1971), p. 158.

[5]Gerard Manley Hopkins, "God's Grandeur."

[6]Jonathan Edwards, *Religious Affections* (Grand Rapids, Mich., 1982), p. 199.

[7]Ibid., p. 14.

[8]Ibid.

[9]À Kempis, *Imitation of Christ*, p. 136.

Chapter 8: Being a Dragon Slayer

[1]Jon Johnston, "Making Excellence Christian," *Evangelical Newsletter*, vol. 12, no. 22, 1985.